OCS Study MMS 2005-062

Final Report

Title: Susceptibility of sea ice biota to disturbances in the shallow Beaufort Sea: Phase 1: Biological coupling of sea ice with the pelagic and benthic realms

Rolf R Gradinger – Principal Investigator
Bodil A Bluhm – Co-principal Investigator

November 2005

Table of Contents

Summary

We assessed the impact of sediment load on the abundances and composition of biological communities in near-shore fast ice and underlying waters close to Barrow, Alaska. Based on existing scientific evidence we hypothesized that any disturbance of the sea ice habitat, e.g. by enhanced sediment load, construction of ice roads and gas or oil spills, would likely impact the biological links between ice, water column and sea floor and may, hence, affect the biomass and productivity in all realms. Sampling was conducted in April 2002 and February, April and May 2003 with ice corers, water samplers, plankton nets and sediment corers at two locations which differed mainly in terms of sea ice sediment load. In 2003 a strong ice algal bloom developed in the sediment-free fast ice, reaching a maximum pigment concentration of 330 µg Chl a l^{-1} in the bottom 10cm of the ice in May while it remained below 1µg Chl a l^{-1} in the water column. With increasing ice algal biomass, the $\delta^{13}C$ ratio of sea ice POM increased from an initial average value of -25‰ in February to -16‰ in May, while no enrichment was observed in pelagic POM. The abundance of ice metazoans increased with the progressing season to a maximum of 276,000 animals m^{-2}, dominated by nematodes and merosympagic polychaete juveniles. Abundances of meroplanktic stages of benthic polychaetes in the water column were consistently at least one order of magnitude below abundances in the ice, suggesting sea ice as an important feeding habitat for young life stages. The sediment loaded sea ice had a total particle load of 106 g m^{-2}. Light was reduced by more than 99% compared to the clean ice site, which had a particle load of only 6 g m^{-2}. In the dirty ice we observed no substantial increase, over time, for any of the studied biological parameters. Our observations demonstrate that sea ice sediments have a profound impact on sea ice biology, suppressing biological spring bloom formation by orders of magnitude compared to clean ice. Stable isotope analyses of ice meiofauna and gut/stomach content analyses on amphipods supported the concept of sea ice algae being important food in Arctic coastal food webs in early spring. The study progress and results were communicated to the community in Barrow through public presentations, radio and newspaper contributions. The science community was informed through conference presentations, publications and web pages.

Background

Sea ice is a key component in structuring polar environments (Eicken 1992, Sakshaug 1991, Gradinger & Spindler 1997, Gradinger 2002). Beside its important role as a platform for marine mammals and birds, it serves as a habitat for a unique highly specialized community of bacteria, algae, protozoa and metazoa, which contribute to the biogeochemical cycles of the Arctic and Antarctic seas. Early seal hunters had already discovered the close relationship between ice algae production and higher trophic levels when they found numerous seals associated with brownish-colored ice floes which they, therefore, named *seal-ice* (Nansen 1897). This coloration is caused by billions of unicellular algae living within the sea ice. The ice algal primary production in seasonally ice-covered waters contributes 4 to 26% of total primary production (Legendre et al. 1992) and may even be above 50% in the permanently ice-covered central Arctic (Gosselin et al. 1997) due to the low amount of short wave radiation penetrating into the water column (Gosselin et al. 1997). The few available time series data reported a seasonal variability by a factor of ~10 for algal and bacterial biomass, and >50 for primary and bacterial production (Horner 1980, Smith et al. 1988, Gradinger et al. 1991, Haecky & Andersson 1999). A significant fraction of the spatial and temporal variability is directly linked to environmental variables, in particular light availability and nutrient supply. These are modulated by snow cover, ice morphology and ice microstructure (Sullivan et al. 1985, Gosselin et al. 1986, Eicken et al. 1991, Gradinger et al. 1991, Legendre et al. 1991, Gradinger 1999a). The locally enormous sediment load of so-called "dirty ice" (e.g., Reimnitz et al. 1987, Nürnberg et al. 1994, Eicken et al. in press) is assumed to have an additional, profound impact on the ice biota through alteration of the available light energy, but this impact has not been quantified yet.

In the coastal Chukchi and Beaufort Seas, mass developments of unicellular algae of maximum concentrations of $43*10^6$ cells l^{-1} ice (Horner 1976) were reported in the bottom layers of the fast ice in spring (May/June). Both the plant biomass and plant productivity inside the ice out-reach the water column values during this period of the year. The only available estimate of annual ice algal primary production is 5gC m^{-2} for the shallow Beaufort Sea (Alexander 1974), which is in the range of data from other coastal locations with an annual ice cover (Arrigo 2003). Horner's summary (1984) of the knowledge of ice algal biomass and production is still the most recent publication on the topic in the Beaufort Sea area.

Recent changes were observed in Arctic ice extent and thickness (e.g. Parkinson et al. 1999, Rothrock et al. 1999), and model results (e.g., Gordon & O'Farrell 1997) predict a 60% loss in summer sea ice extent in the northern hemisphere by the time atmospheric CO_2 has doubled. Results from the SHEBA ice drift experiment already point toward substantial changes in the ice community composition during ice melt with freshwater algae being dominant and sea ice fauna completely missing, compared to earlier data (Melnikov et al. 2001). The general scarcity of ice algal biomass data highlights the need for comparative and supplementary new data on ice algal biomass in the Beaufort Sea as acknowledged in the ACIA (2004) report.

Sea ice algae not only contribute significantly to the overall primary production of the Arctic, but they also form the basis for the sea-ice related food web which extends to higher trophic levels, such as sea floor dwellers, seals and polar bears. Carey and co-workers (e.g. Carey & Boudrias 1987, Carey 1992) found high abundances of amphipods, especially *Pseudalibrotus* (=*Onisimus*) *litoralis*, under the Beaufort Sea fast ice. The authors estimated that about 1–10% of the annual ice algal production is grazed by these amphipods and sink, as fecal pellets, to the sea floor where they become available to benthic species. Apart from amphipods, a large assemblage of meiofauna inhabits the sea ice and the ice/water interface, e.g. copepods, copepod nauplii, nematodes, turbellarians, and larvae of benthic polychaetes and gastropods (Carey & Montagna 1982, Cross 1982, Kern & Carey 1983, Grainger et al. 1985, Gradinger 1999b). Grainger and Hsiao (1990) observed that several of these taxa fed on a variety of ice algae in the Canadian Frobisher Bay in early and late spring. The authors concluded that herbivory on ice algae is the dominant feeding mode for ice related meiofauna. To what extent these taxa utilize or even depend on the ice as a food source in the Beaufort Sea and transfer, via the food web, energy from the sea ice to the benthic realm is unknown, especially as to the spatial and temporal variability. The sea ice, pelagic and benthic realms are, moreover, coupled through the complex life cycles of their inhabitants. The studies in the shallow coastal Beaufort Sea (summarized by Carey 1992) suggest that larvae of benthic copepods, polychaetes and gastropods use sea ice as a nursery ground, whereas the adults of these taxa inhabit the benthos.

Ratios of naturally occurring stable isotopes of carbon δ^{13}C and nitrogen (δ^{15}N) are widely used in identifying food web connections in Arctic and other marine ecosystems (e.g. Hobson & Welch 1992, Iken et al. 2005). Both carbon and nitrogen ratios increase from one trophic level to the next in known steps (Fry & Sherr 1988) – for δ^{13}C with a typical increase of 1‰, for δ^{15}N with an increase of 3–4‰. This enrichment, an increasing contribution of the heavier isotope ^{13}C and ^{15}N, is caused by preferred physiological processing (e.g. respiration, excretion) of the lighter isotopes (^{12}C and ^{14}N). Identifying trophic interactions based on field stable isotope data is dependent on knowing the isotopic signature of the carbon source, the marine primary producers. Isotopic ratios for marine primary producers can change on large scales (e.g. with latitude) but also within one region depending on habitat. The differences between isotopic ratios of, for example, primary producers in the benthic environment and in the pelagic environment can be used to follow the fate of these production units in the marine food web. Large differences in the isotopic signature have been reported for sea ice algae and polar phytoplankton in general, with ice algae being isotopically heavier (higher δ^{13}C ratios) than phytoplankton (Hobson et al. 1995). The heavier δ^{13}C isotopic signature of ice algae is caused by the limited availability of inorganic carbon within the brine channel network (Kennedy et al. 2002, Thomas & Papadimitriou 2003). In conclusion, the variation in isotopic ratios of organic material in polar waters can be attributed to two major factors: a) habitat specific ratios for primary producers (e.g. ice algae versus phytoplankton) and b) changes due to food web interactions (e.g. herbivores versus carnivores).

The previously described studies provide windows of insight into some of the principle coupling processes between sea ice, water column and benthos. Although many questions remain open, the results show that a wide variety of taxa spend at least a certain part of their lives in or associated with sea ice and may depend on the provided food source and habitat. Hence, any disturbance of the sea ice habitat, e.g. by enhanced sediment load, construction of ice roads and gas or oil spills, would likely impact the biological links between ice, water column and sea floor and may, hence, affect the biomass and productivity in all realms. Some of these disturbances operate by decreasing the amount of light available to primary producers while others affect the water chemistry. The possibility of such disturbances is increasing with the present acceleration of oil and gas exploration and development in the Arctic shelf seas, such as the Beaufort Sea.

Over the last 15 years, several studies focused on the disturbance under sea ice by an oil spill. In Antarctic sea ice, crude oil and diesel fuel negatively impacted ice algal biomass (Fiala & Delille 1999) whereas no adverse effects were observed in an ice algae community after a short-term exposure to oil during the Baffin Island Oil Spill (BIOS) experiment (Cross 1987). While the risk of larger oil spills in the shallow Beaufort Sea is considered to be low (MMS 2001), an increase in sediment load in the water column and the sea ice, and eventually on the sea floor, is undoubtedly linked to exploration-related construction work. Trenching for oil pipelines, hauling gravel for road or island constructions and water discharge, including particulate matter, are typical activities that will enhance the load of particulate matter in the marine environment (MMS 2001). Suspended sediments are incorporated into sea ice by various naturally occurring processes during ice formation, similar to the incorporation of ice organisms (Reimnitz et al. 1992, Gradinger & Ikävalko 1998) and are released at ice melt. Light, obviously, is the dominant factor controlling the seasonality of plant production in polar environments. Field and experimental data showed a strong decrease of ice algal abundance and productivity with increasing snow thickness caused by light reduction (e.g. Gradinger et al. 1991). Incorporated sea ice sediments will further reduce light levels by increased attenuation, which will most likely further reduce production and accumulation rates of ice algae. High turbidity will also reduce planktonic and, thus, benthic primary and secondary production, but quantitative studies on this topic are scarce. MMS (2001) assessed the potential negative impact on the production of macrophytes in the Beaufort Sea boulder patch to be in the order of 6%.

Our proposed work aimed at contributing to "*better understanding coastal marine environments affected by offshore oil and gas exploration*" (CMI framework issue 1) in coastal Alaskan waters.

Based on existing knowledge of the linkages between sea ice and adjacent habitats as well as on potential effects of disturbances, we addressed the following major hypotheses: (1) Sea ice biota contributes significantly to the biogeochemical cycle in the fast ice-covered shallow Beaufort Sea in terms of production of organic material and also as a seasonal habitat and food source for pelagic and benthic invertebrates, (2) Certain life stages of a number of benthic taxa depend on the ice algal biomass as a food source early in the year prior to the occurrence of phytoplankton blooms, and (3) Disturbances of the linkages between sea ice, water column and benthos will reduce the abundance of ice associated biota.

Our objectives were:
a) to determine the diversity, abundance and biomass of ice related fauna in comparison to planktonic and benthic communities in relation to ice sediment load,
b) to determine algal biomass in the sea ice, water column and benthos to assess the absolute and relative amount of available food in sea ice in relation to sediment load and

c) to identify the relevance of sea ice-produced organic material for the nearshore food web, based on stable isotope analysis.

Study area

The fast ice along the Alaskan coastline forms in November/December and reaches a thickness of 1.5–1.8m by April (Macdonald et al. 1999, Gradinger & Bluhm 2003). Break-up usually occurs between late June and mid-July. Attached to the shore and anchored to the sea floor by up to 20–25 m deep keels (Macdonald 2000), the ice extends several km out onto the Chukchi and Beaufort shelves. We chose the fast ice cover close to Barrow, Alaska as the study area (Fig. 1), as the Barrow Arctic Science Consortium's (BASC) logistics provide easy access to the ice, and earlier studies had demonstrated the formation of pronounced algal blooms in sediment-free fast ice in this area (Horner & Schrader 1982).

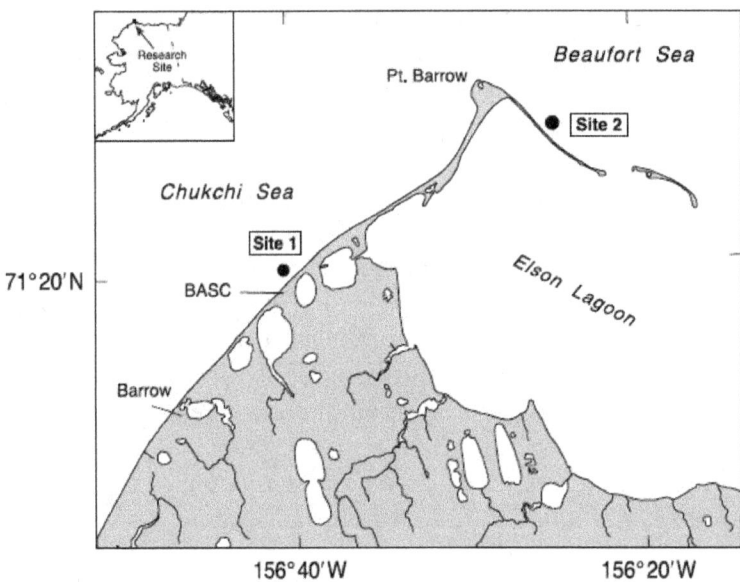

Figure 1: Location map at the northernmost tip of Alaska. BASC = Barrow Arctic Science Consortium. Site 1: no sediment, Site 2: substantial sediment load in sea ice.

Sampling was conducted April 24–28, 2002 and February 12–17, April 1–5 and May 27–30, 2003. The fast ice was sampled in level, un-ridged areas. The first sampling in April 2002 was used to collect sediment-free ice at both locations to detect potential site-specific differences. Site 1 (Fig 1, 2a and c) was chosen based on its easy access in all weather conditions, while site 2 (Fig. 1, 2b) provided a higher likelihood of encountering sediment in the sea ice. Site 1 (without visible sediment incorporation in both years) was located in the Chukchi Sea just offshore of the BASC facilities (71° 20′N, 156° 42′W). Site 2, located around Point Barrow in the Beaufort Sea (71° 22′N, 156° 24′W) exhibited a substantial amount of sediment in the top 40 to 44 cm in 2003 (Fig 2b: gray layer at top of ice core). Both sites were approximately 200 m offshore in a water depth of 5 to 5.6 m.

Figure 2: Field view of sites 1 (a) and 2 (b). Note the substantial amount of sediment in the top 40–44 cm of the ice core at site 2. Both pictures were taken during the February 2003 field campaign. c) Examples of the sampling gear used for the study.

The fieldwork is documented on the project's web page:
http://www.sfos.uaf.edu/research/seaicebiota/cmi/barrow2002/index.html.

Material and Methods

During each field phase, we collected samples from the sea ice, the water column and the sea floor at two fast ice locations close to Barrow (Fig. 2a, c for examples of sampling gear used).

At each location, snow thickness was determined at ten locations in a perimeter of 1 m around the site. Air, snow surface, snow/ice interface and ice temperatures were measured with a Traceable thermometer (accuracy of 0.05°K). Ice cores were collected with a KOVACS-type ice auger (10 cm diameter) and the total ice thickness was recorded from a minimum of four cores per site. One complete core from each site was melted to determine total sediment load. Ice temperature was measured immediately after coring on one ice core per site in 10 to 20 cm intervals over the entire ice thickness. Temperature and salinity (T/S) of the water column were determined with a YSI 85 sensor at 1 m intervals. Freezing within the T/S sensor head due to cold surface temperatures (down to -30°C) caused malfunction of the salinity readings in February and April 2003.

At each station and date, the PAR (photosynthetically active radiation: 400–700 nm wavelength) intensity was measured with a LI-COR underwater 4π spherical sensor at 1 m intervals through a separate core hole. A 2π planar sensor that remained on the ice surface provided a reference. To ensure accurate depth readings, for both light and T/S, the sensors were attached to marked fiberglass rods. Light measurements were conducted around solar noon. Both sensors measured the photon quantum flux density (number of photons per unit area per unit time, units: μmol photons m^{-2} s^{-1}).

In May 2003, the spectral composition of the incoming radiation on the surface of the sea ice and the downwelling radiation under the sea ice were determined using a calibrated OceanOptics radiometer equipped with a 3 m long fiber-optic cable, to a spectral resolution of 2 nm.

Biological samples were taken from sea ice, water column and sea floor sediment in replicates of four per site, season and parameter, unless otherwise specified.

A minimum of eight ice cores were taken at each site, comprising four replicates of two core sets (A and B). The distance between replicate cores varied between 0.3–2 m. For further processing, we used the bottom 10 cm of the ice cores, as these generally contain the highest ice algal and ice meiofauna abundances (Horner 1985), which was consistent with our visual inspection of all cores sampled. We also verified this assumption in April 2003: 93% of total ice algal biomass (as estimated by the concentrations of the pigment chlorophyll *a*) was located in the bottom 10 cm section of one core taken at site 1 (for details see results section).

The bottom sections of set A of the replicate cores were melted directly in the dark. After complete melt, 50 ml sub-samples were filtered onto Whatman GF/F filters and subsequently frozen for ice algal pigment analysis (Chl *a* and phaeophytin) to estimate biomass. Phaeophytin is a break-down product of chlorophyll and high relative contributions of phaeophytin are indicative of cell mortality/aging of organic material due to grazing or extreme environmental stress, for example. Another set of 50 ml sub-samples was filtered onto pre-combusted and pre-weighed GF/F filters, rinsed and frozen for later determination of stable isotope composition (δ^{13}C, δ^{15}N) and amount of particulate organic carbon and nitrogen (POC, PON).

The bottom sections of core set B were melted in the dark after addition of 1 l each of 0.2 µm-filtered seawater to avoid osmotic stress for the biota. After complete melt, sub-samples of 50 to 200 ml were fixed with 1% formaldehyde for ice algal counts to estimate abundances (cell count per ml). The remaining samples were concentrated over 20 µm gauze. Metazoan ice meiofauna was sorted and counted fresh or after fixation in 4% formaldehyde using a Wild M3 dissecting microscope to estimate abundances. All counts were corrected for dilution factors.

Water samples were taken through the core holes from an intermediate water depth (3 m) with a Kemmerer water sampler. For analysis of phytoplankton biomass (Chl a and phaeophytin), POC, PON and stable isotope composition (δ^{13}C, δ^{15}N), 0.2–0.5 l each was filtered on GF/F filters and treated like the ice samples. For phytoplankton cell counts, subsamples of 200 ml were fixed with 1% formaldehyde to estimate phytoplankton abundances.

The major tool for processing the particle samples in the sea ice algae and phytoplankton size range was a FLOWCAM, an image analysis-based flow-cytometer. Three digital pictures per second were recorded from the continuous sample stream and were simultaneously analyzed for particle abundance and size. Absolute particle abundances were calculated based on the mean number of particles per image and a minimum count of 200 particles per sample. The digital images of the individual particles were used to identify the particle composition within each selected size fraction (5 to <10 µm, 10 to < 20 µm and ≥20 µm). Four samples per site and sampling period were analyzed from the sea ice and the water column.

Vertical zooplankton hauls were taken with 20 µm and 200 µm nets. Samples were sorted either live or after preservation in formaldehyde (4% final concentration), and specimens were counted by taxon using a dissecting microscope to estimate zooplankton abundance.

Benthic sediment samples were collected with a benthic corer (6 cm diameter) with an attached extension deployed through a core hole. The top 5 cm of the cores were collected, thoroughly mixed, and sub-samples were frozen for determination of algal biomass in sea floor sediments.

Algal pigments were extracted from samples from all three realms. Ice algal and phytoplankton samples were extracted with 7 ml of 90% acetone for 24 hours in the freezer (Gradinger et al. 2005). In the case of the sea floor sediment algae samples, 15 ml of 90% acetone were added to approximately 1 g (wet weight) of sediment (Conde et al. 1999). After extraction of the sediment samples, 7 ml of acetone were transferred into a borosilicate tube and centrifuged for 20 minutes at 1500 min[-1]. Pigment concentrations (Chlorophyll a and phaeophytin) were determined fluorometrically with a Turner Designs fluorometer (Arar & Collins 1992). Following the pigment extraction, the sediment was dried at 60°C for 24 hours and weighed. Chlorophyll (Chl) a concentrations in sediment are therefore presented per g dry weight sediment.

Filters for stable isotope analysis were dried in a drying oven at 65°C for 1–2 days and subsequently weighed for total dry weight to determine total load of particulate matter (POC, PON). All filters were then HCl-fumed (to remove carbonates) in a vacuum chamber for 24 hours and dried again. The filters were folded into tin cups and delivered to the University of Alaska Fairbanks (UAF) Stable Isotope Facility where they were run on ThermoFinnigan Delta mass spectrometers for their $\delta^{13}C$ and $\delta^{15}N$ values and particulate organic carbon (POC) and nitrogen (PON) masses. Sample isotopic ratios are expressed in the conventional notation as parts per thousand (‰) according to the following equation:

$$\delta X = [(R_{sample}/R_{standard}) - 1] \cdot 1000$$

where X is ^{13}C or ^{15}N of the sample and R is the corresponding ratio $^{13}C/^{12}C$ or $^{15}N/^{14}N$. Terminology being used when presenting isotope data is: enriched=heavier (containing more of the heavy isotope) and depleted=lighter (containing less of the heavy isotope). Enrichment in $\delta^{13}C$ results in fewer negative numbers; enrichment in $\delta^{15}N$ results in more positive numbers. For a single sample, 0.2–0.4 mg dry mass of faunal tissue are required at current equipment sensitivity. Depending on the body mass of a species/taxon, this amount required pooling up to several hundred individuals, e.g. 30–50 turbellarians, 50–80 polychaete juveniles, 150–300 copepod nauplii or nematodes. Due to the considerable effort required to pick this amount from a sample and due to low faunal densities in the winter and/or site 2, samples could only be obtained from taxa that were reasonably common at a site at any given time.

Gut and stomach content analyses were performed on amphipods collected in traps (Fig. 2a), that had been deployed under the sea ice for time periods of up to 24 hours in February, April and May 2003. Stomachs and guts of three randomly selected animals from each sampling date and site were placed on a microscope slide and microscopically examined at a magnification of 400x using a ZEISS compound microscope. The particle composition in the stomachs/guts was qualitatively analyzed in terms of size of particles and occurrence of identifiable biological material. Digital pictures were taken with a Canon Rebel digital camera at highest resolution and were enhanced using GraphicConverter.

Means, standard deviations, Kendall and Spearman rank correlations and various tests for differences between the observations at site 1 and site 2 were calculated using the following software packages: Excel, Kaleidagraph, Systat and Statview.

Results

Physical properties

Over the course of the study, the snow thickness varied within and between sampling events and stations between 3 and 7 cm. A major ice break-off had occurred at site 1 on December 23, 2002. Therefore, ice thickness at that site was lower (0.8 m) than at site 2 (1.2 m) in February 2003. Ice thickness increased over time to maximum values of 1.3 m at site 1 and 1.7 m at site 2 in May 2003. The variability of ice thickness at each site at each sampling event was less than 5 cm.

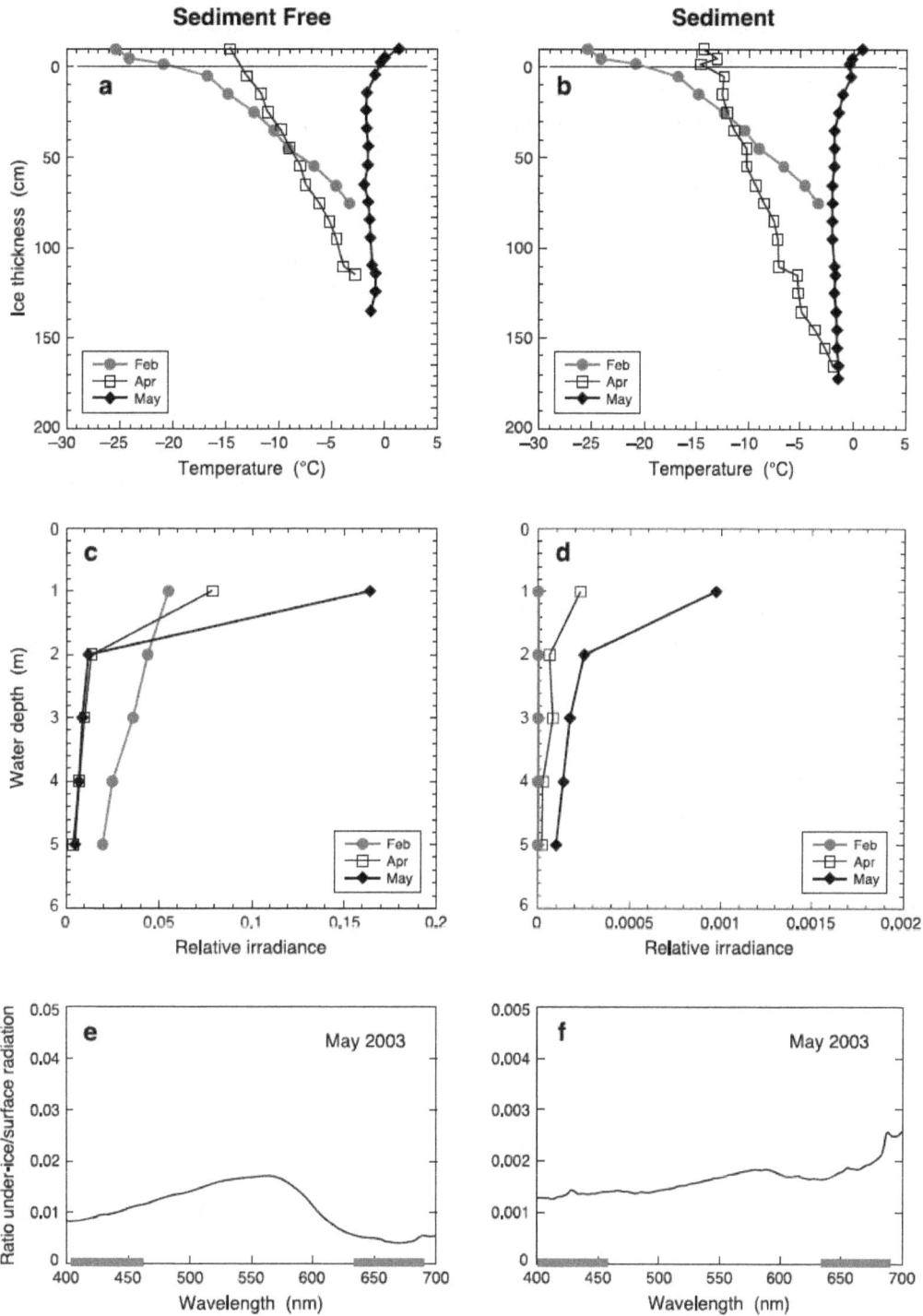

Figure 3: Environmental parameters (temperature and irradiance) at site 1 (with no sediment, left) and site 2 (high sediment load, right) in sea ice cover in 2003. a and b: Sea ice temperatures. Horizontal line indicates top of ice floe; measurements above the line were made in air and snow. c and d: Sub-ice irradiance (ratio 4π under-water to 2π surface sensor). e and f: Spectral light composition in May 2003. Thick gray lines along the x-axis indicate ranges of maximum chlorophyll absorption. Note the different scales for site 1 and 2 for some parameters.

The temperatures in the ice cores were coldest at the top and decreased to seawater temperature at the bottom. The temperature gradient and its seasonal change within the ice were very similar at the two sites (Fig. 3a and b). The coldest air and ice temperatures were encountered in February 2003, with minimum ice temperatures of -25°C at the ice surface and air temperatures of -30°C. Ice temperatures in April 2003 ranged from -13°C at the top of the ice cores to -1.9°C in the lowermost 10cm. In late May, ice temperatures had increased to -0.2 to -2°C at the ice surface. A slight temperature increase with season was also detectable in the temperature readings closest to the ice-water interface from -4.5°C in February to -1.9°C in April and -1.4°C in May 2003. The temperature profiles in the water column (not shown) exhibited neither seasonal patterns nor any indication of vertical stratification. Values ranged between -1.4 and -2°C. Salinity (not shown) in May varied between 30.6 and 31.9.

The incident short wave radiation in the PAR range increased with season at sites 1 and 2 from February (34 and 138 µmol photons $m^{-2} s^{-1}$) to April (393 and 642 µmol photons $m^{-2} s^{-1}$) to May (886 and 1402 µmol photons $m^{-2} s^{-1}$). Light intensities at the ice/water interface under sediment-loaded sea ice (site 2) were two orders of magnitude below those under sediment-free ice (site 1; Fig. 3c and d), and never exceeded an absolute value of 0.4 µmol photons $m^{-2} s^{-1}$. At site 1, the relative irradiance levels in the ice/water interface region decreased from February to April and remained low in May. Distinct differences between sea ice with a high sediment load (site 2) versus low sediment load (site 1) were evident in the spectral light composition (Fig. 3e and f). At site 1, attenuation was highest in the blue and red wave bands, where the algal pigment chlorophyll has its absorbance maxima. In contrast, the spectral composition at site 2 did not indicate any preferential absorption in the PAR range (400 to 700 nm).

The dry mass (DM) of particulate matter over the entire ice thickness was 15.3 times higher at site 2 (102.41 g DM m^{-2}) than at site 1 (6.67 g DM m^{-2}) in April 2003. The analysis of the four replicates of the bottom sections revealed that approximately 0.9% of the total particle load was localized in the bottom 10 cm at site 2 (0.9 ± 0.1 g DM m^{-2}), while the fraction at site 1 was considerably higher with 46.5% (3.1 ± 0.9 g DM m^{-2}).

Biological properties

Seasonal changes in ice algal biomass (given as mean Chl a units ± SD) were observed at both sampling locations. At site 1 (without sediment), algal pigment content in the bottom 10 cm of the sea ice increased by two orders of magnitude from February (7.4 ± 0.7 µg Chl a l^{-1}) to May 2003 (329.3 ± 42.0 µg Chl a l^{-1} sea ice) (Fig. 4a). In the dirty sea ice at site 2, pigment concentration increased slightly from 1.9 ± 0.0 µg Chl a l^{-1} in February to 8.3 ± 7.0 µg Chl a l^{-1} in May 2003. Pigment levels at site 2 had been higher than at site 1 in April 2002, when only clean ice had been collected from both sites. The Chl a/phaeophytin ratios decreased at both locations with progressing season from February (13.3 ± 1.7 at site 1, and 10.3 ± 4.9 at site 2) to May (6.3 ± 1.3 at site 1, and 2.7 ± 0.8 at site 2). Analysis of algal pigment concentration at site 1 over the entire ice thickness in April 2003 demonstrated that the bottom 10 cm contained 93% (7.72 mg

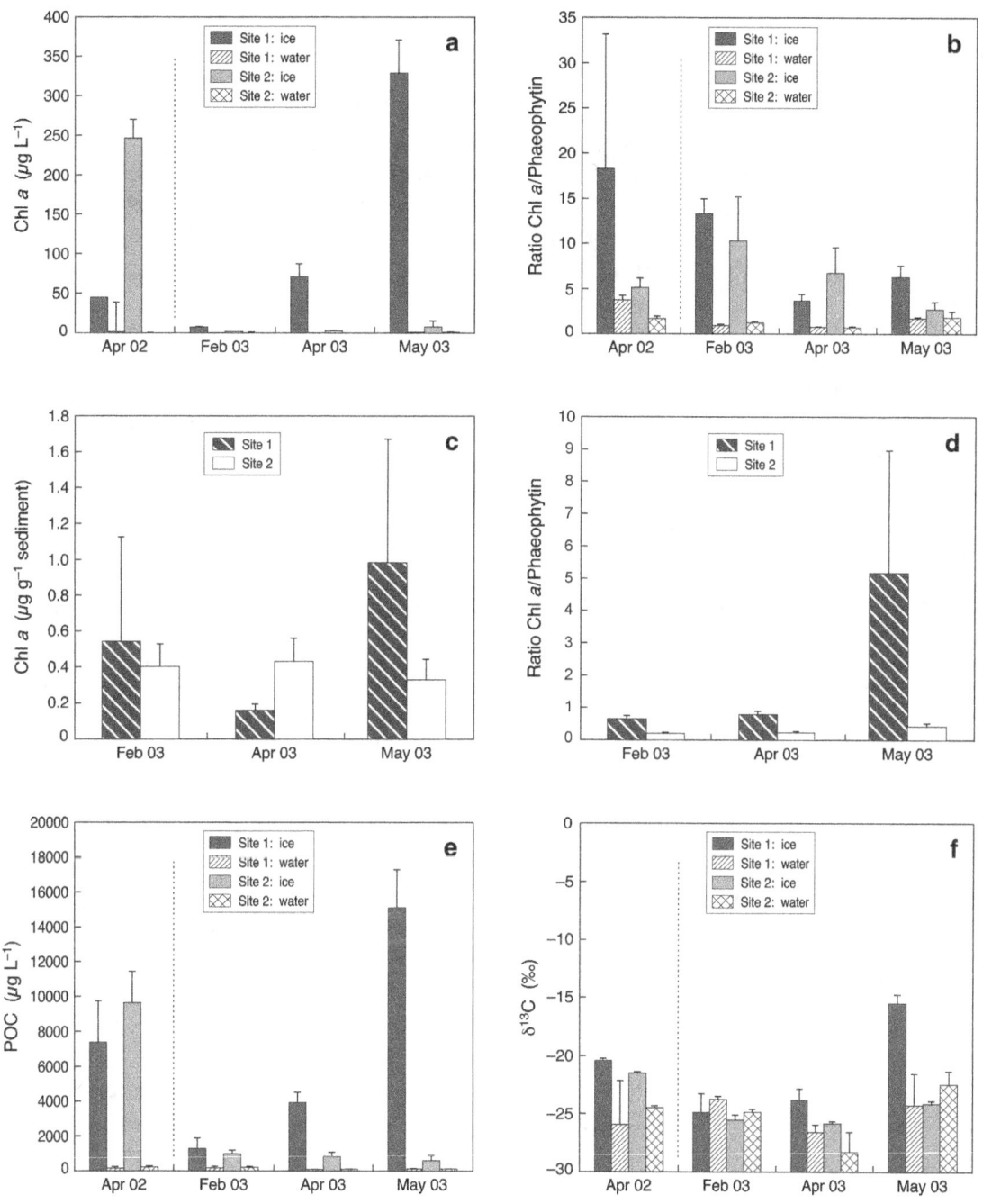

Figure 4: Particulate organic carbon (POC), and algal pigment concentrations and ratios at two coastal fast ice sites with no sediment (site 1) and high sediment load (site 2) during sea ice cover in 2003. Algal pigment concentrations (a and c) and pigment ratios (Chl *a*/phaeophytin; b and d) in ice, water and sediment. POC and δ^{13}C (e and f) in sea ice and water samples.

Chl a m^{-2}) of the entire integrated pigment content (8.31 mg Chl a m^{-2}) (Fig. 5). Visual inspection revealed no indication of internal or surface pigment maxima in any of the other cores taken throughout the project. The chlorophyll increase at site 1 over the 103 days between the February and May sampling converts into a net algal doubling time of 18.8 days, while the algal doubling time at site 2 (with sediment, 49 days) was higher compared to site 1 by a factor of 2.6.

Compared to sea ice algal concentrations, phytoplankton pigment levels remained low (< 2 µg Chl a l^{-1}) throughout the 2003 study period at both locations (Fig. 4a). The Chl a/phaeophytin ratios at the two sites were lowest in April 2003 (0.7 ± 0.1) and highest in late May 2003 (1.8 ± 0.6) with no significant site-specific differences (Fig. 4b). The ratio of the mean Chl a concentrations in sea ice relative to the water column increased with the progressing season from 150 (February) to 370 (May) at site 1, while it decreased from 47 to 9 at site 2.

Mean benthic sediment chlorophyll concentrations varied between <0.2 and >1.0 µg Chl a g^{-1} DM (dry mass) sediment throughout the sampling period at both sites, with no clear seasonal trend at site 2, but a mean increase at site 1 in May (Fig. 4c). The pigment concentrations in the sea floor sediment varied considerably between replicates at site 1. Reasons for the high variability may relate to the difficulty in sampling the coarse sea floor sediment. Chl a/phaeophytin ratios remained below 0.9 ± 0.4 at site 2 with no clear seasonal pattern. A dramatic increase occurred in May at site 1 (5.2 ± 3.8, Fig. 4d).

Ice algae and phytoplankton are the main contributors to living particulate organic carbon (POC) together with detritus, bacteria and proto- and metazoans. The sea ice POC concentrations increased at site 1 by a factor of 12 during the 2003 sampling period (Fig. 4e) from 1.3 ± 0.6 mg l^{-1} in February to 15.2 ± 1.9 mg POC l^{-1} in May. At site 2, POC decreased from February (9.8 ± 2.2 mg l^{-1}) to May (5.7 ± 4.3 mg l^{-1}). POC concentrations in the water column remained below 0.2 mg l^{-1} at both sites throughout the study period.

At site 1, δ^{13}C became increasingly enriched (less negative) with the progressing season from -24.9 ± 1.6‰ in February to -15.5 ± 0.8‰ in May (Fig. 4f). In contrast, the isotopic signature remained below -25‰ at site 2 in February and April and got slightly enriched to -24.2 ± 0.2 ‰ in May. The positive relationship between δ^{13}C (‰) and POC (µg/l) was highly significant:

(1) δ^{13}C = -25.964 + 0.0007*POC (r^2 = 0.899, n=18, p<0.0001).

At both sites, stable isotope ratios in the water column samples were depleted in April (-26.6 ± 0.7‰ at site 1, -28.3 ± 1.7‰ at site 2) relative to February (site 1: -23.8 ± 0.3‰, site 2: -24.9 ± 0.3‰) and May (site 1: -24.3 ± 2.7‰, site 2: -22.5 ± 1.2‰).

The abundance of ice algae in cells/ml (for examples of FLOWCAM pictures see Fig. 6) increased strongly at site 1 from February to May in 2003 (mean values ±

standard deviations: Fig. 7). Large single-celled ice diatoms such as the one shown in Fig. 8a dominated the size fraction ≥20 μm in May 2003 in all clean ice cores (Fig. 6f), while they were nearly absent from all other samples (e.g., Fig. 6c). The growth (=cell division) of ice diatoms caused the significant increase in particle numbers in this size fraction at site 1 between February and May, while no such change was seen in the dirty sea ice at site 2 or in the phytoplankton samples (Fig. 7). This observation is consistent with the relative changes in chlorophyll a and particulate organic carbon concentrations.

The abundance of meiofauna (examples in Fig. 8) within the bottom 10cm section of the sea ice, cores followed the changes of the ice algal biomass (Fig. 9a and b). At site 1, mean total abundance increased from 18,000 individuals m^{-2} sea ice in February to 276,000 individuals m^{-2} in May. In contrast, mean total abundances at site 2 remained below 17,000 individuals m^{-2} throughout the study period in 2003 with no seasonal trend. At both locations, ice meiofauna was dominated by polychaete juveniles, nematodes, copepods (calanoid, cyclopoid and harpacticoid), copepod nauplii and turbellaria (Fig. 8). Taxa less frequently found (listed as others, Fig. 9) were mainly unidentified larvae, rotifers and cnidarians. Unicellular meiofauna taxa (ciliates and flagellates) occurred regularly but were not quantified. High abundance of nematodes in May at site 1 was a result of reproduction: we observed juveniles hatching out of egg cases in the laboratory. We kept a few ice polychaete juveniles from site 1 in culture (12:12h light:dark, -1°C) in the lab in Fairbanks, which as subadults were identified as *Scolelepis squamata* (Spionidae).

Zooplankton abundances in the water column showed a seasonal increase of similar magnitude at both sites in 2003 (Fig. 9c and d). Average values increased from 2,140 individuals m^{-2} at site 1 and 4730 individuals m^{-2} at site two in February to 28,360 individuals m^{-2} at site one and 56,300 individuals m^{-2} at site 2 in May. At all sampling dates, the zooplankton (Fig. 9c and d) was dominated by copepods, with nauplii starting to occur in late April (2002) and May (2003). The total abundance of polychaete juveniles in the water column was <700 individuals m^{-2} at any of the sampling events and, thus, at least one order of magnitude below polychaete juvenile abundances in the sea ice in April and May (3,520 to 136,600 individuals m^{-2}) at site 1.

Collecting quantitative benthic samples was extremely difficult through the ice sheet. The coarse sea floor sediment at site 1 frequently did not stay in the corer during retrieval. We were able to analyze the relative meiofauna composition in one benthic sediment core collected at site 1 in May 2003. The composition was dominated by harpacticoid copepods (28%), other copepods (21%), copepod nauplii (27%), and nematodes (7%); we did not observe polychaete larvae and juveniles in this sample.

Using the means for all parameters of the complete sea ice data set from both sampling sites and all dates, the correlation analysis (Table 1) revealed significant relationships between various ice biota biomass and abundance parameters. Ice algal Chl a and POC were significantly correlated as well as ice meiofauna abundance and ice algal Chl a and POC, respectively. The $\delta^{13}C$ ratios were significantly correlated with Chl a and POC values.

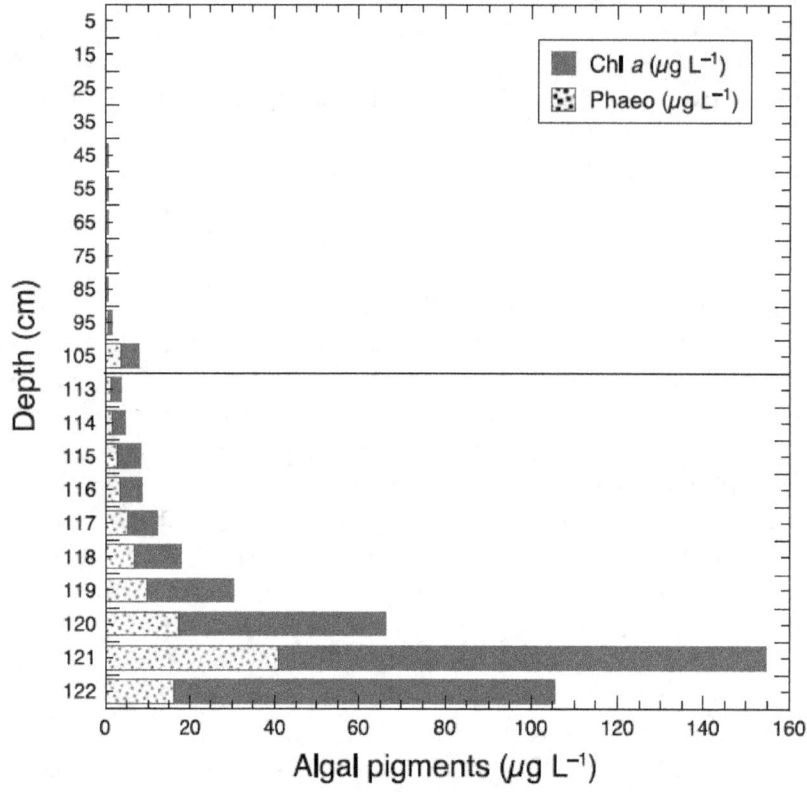

Figure 5: Algal pigment concentration in April 2003 at site 1. Note that the vertical resolution changes from 10 cm sections (top 112 cm) to 1 cm sections in the bottom 10 cm of the core (indicated by the horizontal line). Depth represents the midpoint between the upper and lower end of a section.

$\delta^{13}C$ and $\delta^{15}N$ means (± standard deviations) of all analyzed ice meiofauna and zooplankton for all sampling periods are compiled in tables 2 and 3, respectively. Faunal densities, and therefore the number of isotope samples, were too low to observe any trends in stable isotope data at site 2. Figure 10 shows the distribution of the $\delta^{13}C$ values of the more common taxa by taxonomic groups and sampling periods. At site 1 (Fig. 10a, 11), several ice meiofauna taxa showed progressively enriched $\delta^{13}C$ signatures with progressing season, e.g., by around 7‰ in nematodes and turbellaria.

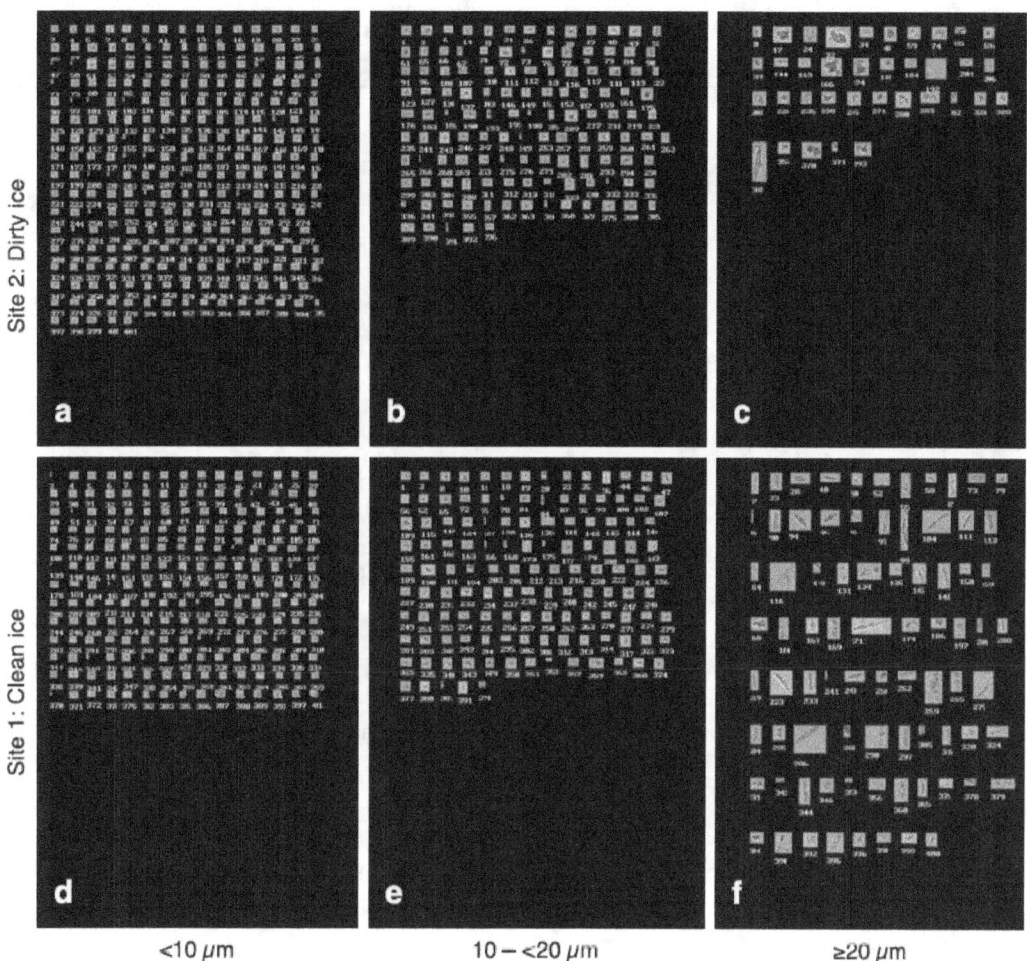

Figure 6: Examples of FLOWCAM images from sea ice samples collected at sites 1 and 2 in May 2003.

A slight enrichment in δ^{13}C occurred in several zooplankton taxa at site 1 (Fig. 10b, 11b), e.g., in nauplii and cyclopoid copepods, while the other sampled taxa revealed no obvious trends. Partial feeding on enriched particles that were released from the sea ice during the first melting processes might explain the enrichment in selected zooplankton taxa late in the sea ice season. Pelagic POM, in contrast, remained rather stable over the time sampled with respect to its carbon isotopic signature and would, therefore, not trigger any isotopic enrichment in its grazers. At site 2, pelagic POM isotope values were more variable between sampling periods while zooplankton signatures showed very little variability.

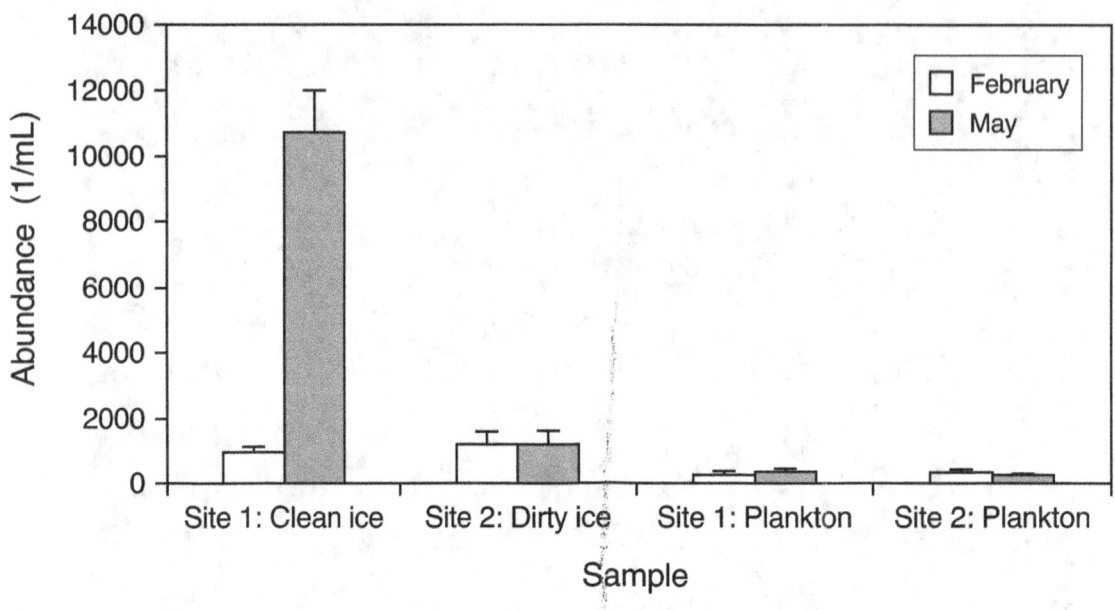

Figure 7: Abundance (N/ml) of particles larger than 20 μm in sea ice and water samples from sites 1 and 2 in 2003. The increase at site 1 is due to growth of sea ice diatoms (see Fig. 6 and 8a).

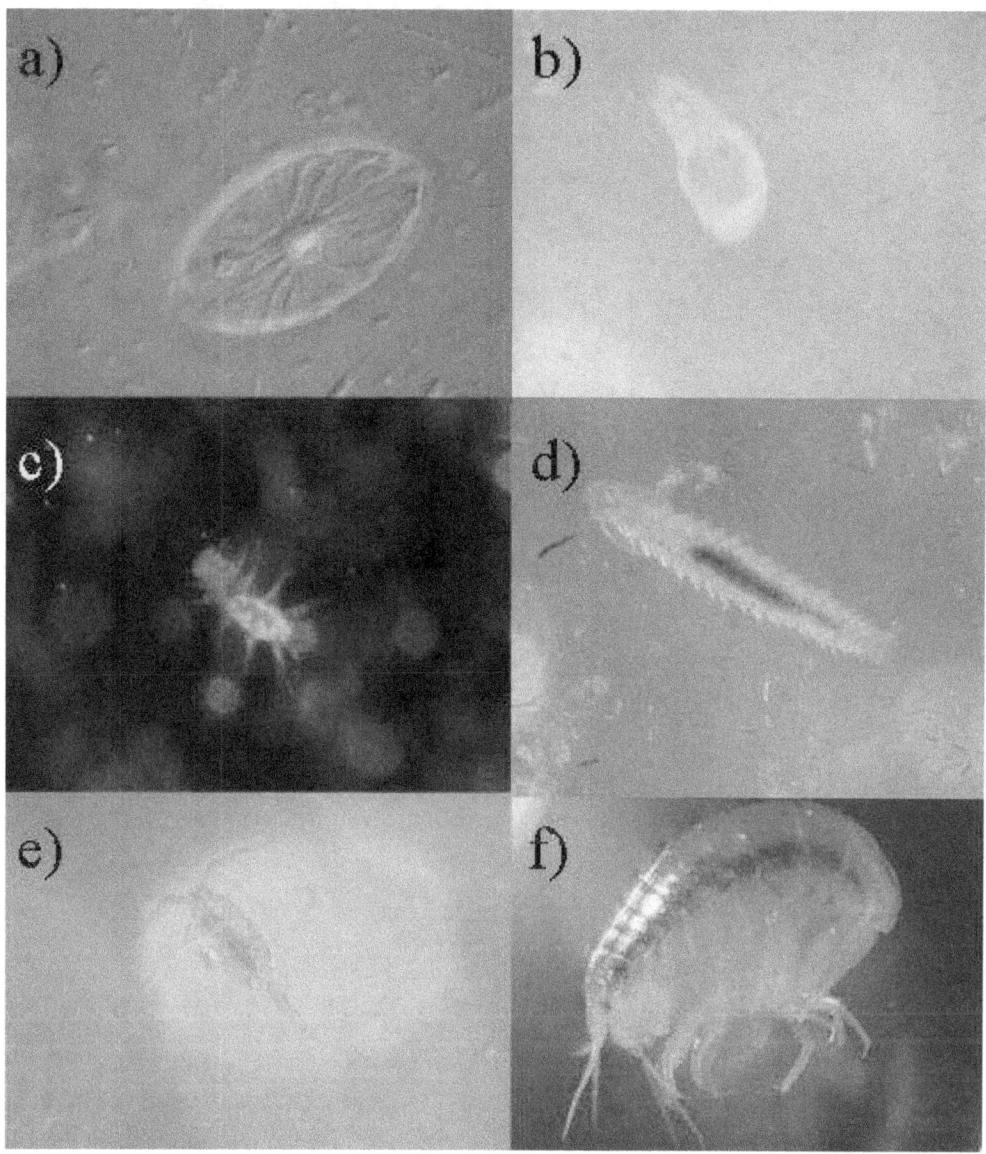

Figure 8: Examples of typical ice inhabiting flora and fauna in the coastal fast ice taken at different magnifications: a) pennate diatom, b) turbellarian, c) polychaete species 1 juvenile (Feb 2003, d) polychaete species 2 juvenile (May 2003), e) copepod *Oithona similis*, f) amphipod *Onisimus glacialis* (sub-ice fauna).

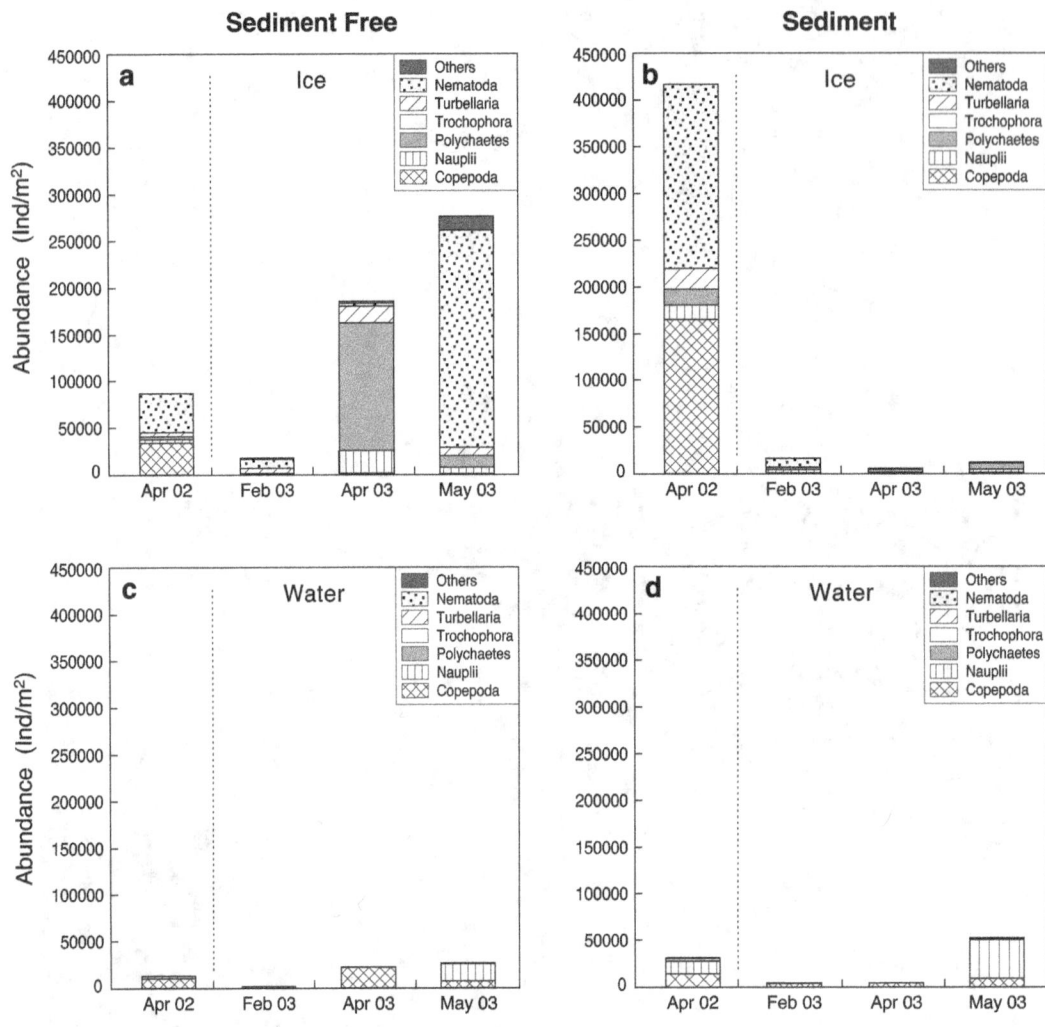

Figure 9: Abundance and composition of metazoans in the sea ice (a and b) and water column (c and d) from April 2002 to May 2003 in and under sediment-free ice (site 1) and sediment-loaded ice (site 2).

Fig. 11 shows the δ^{13}C isotopic signatures for sea ice meiofauna and zooplankton as dependent of the δ^{13}C values of sea ice and pelagic POM (= the carbon sources), respectively. Figure 11a demonstrates a significant positive correlation between sea ice fauna δ^{13}C signatures and ice POM δ^{13}C signatures (Kendall rank correlation test, p=0.04), which, again, suggests a strong dependence of ice fauna on sea ice POM as a food source. At the dirty ice site and for the zooplankton of two sites (Fig. 11), there may also be a positive correlation of faunal δ^{13}C signatures with POM δ^{13}C signatures, at least for zooplankton, but the progressive enrichment of both components with season is not obvious.

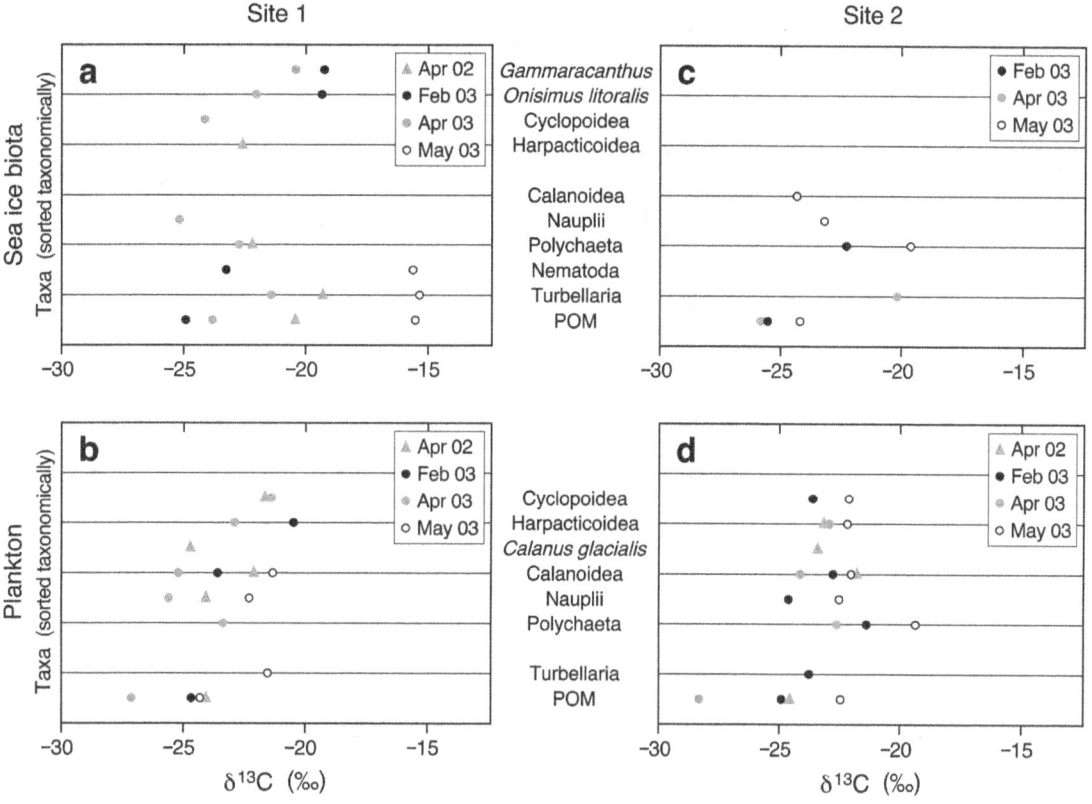

Figure 10: Distribution of δ^{13}C values of sea ice fauna and zooplankton from the Barrow area by taxonomic groups. Sea ice fauna from site 1 (clean ice) (a) and from site 2 (c). Zooplankton from site 1 (b) and from site 2 (d).

The gut content analyses demonstrated a clear shift in the composition of the amphipod food sources. Pennate diatoms, typical for sea ice habitat, were observed in 100% of all fields of view of all animals examined during our study in May, while we observed only one single diatom cell in 60 fields of view studied in three animals collected in February. February stomach and gut contents were dominated by very small particles (<5µm in diameter) with no recognizable biological features. The observations for the April animals revealed intermediate conditions with two animals containing substantial amounts of ice diatoms in its stomach/gut, while the gut/stomach of a third animal was nearly empty with no diatoms observed (Fig. 12).

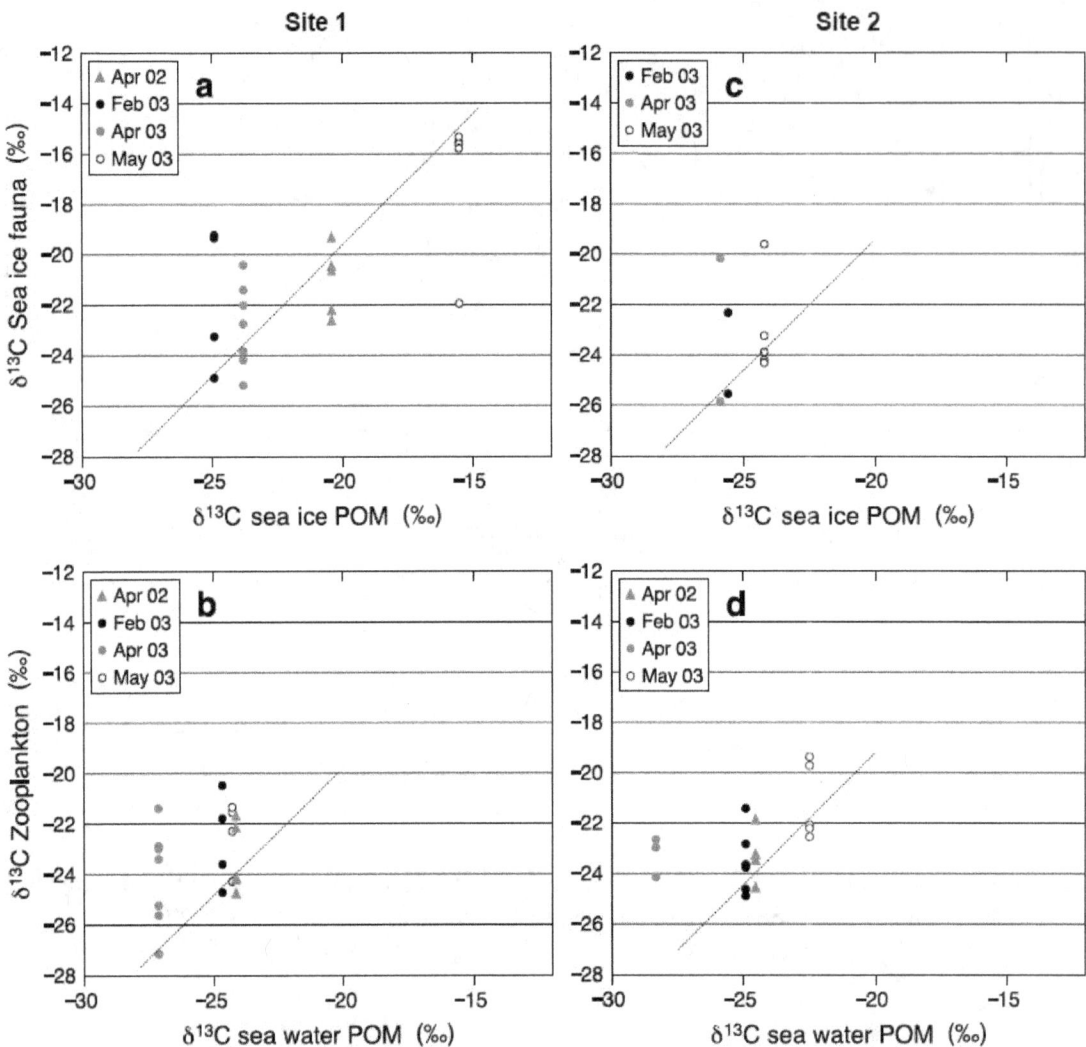

Figure 11: $\delta^{13}C$ isotopic signatures for sea ice meiofauna and zooplankton from sampling sites 1 and 2 for 2002 and 2003 as dependent of the $\delta^{13}C$ values of sea ice and pelagic POM, respectively. Sea ice fauna from site 1 (clean ice) (a) and from site 2 (dirty ice) (c). Zooplankton from site 1 (b) and from site 2 (d). Only the values collected in 2003 are presented in (c) as this was the time of dirty ice at this location. The dashed line indicates a 1:1 relationship.

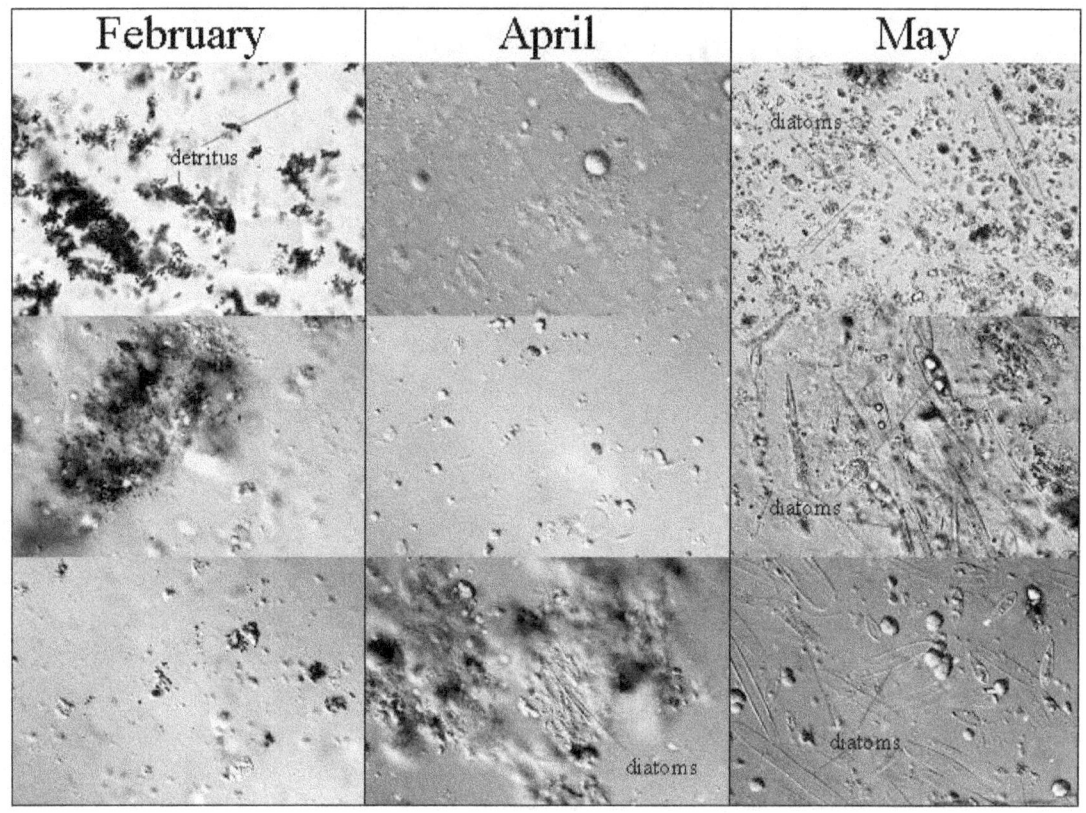

Figure 12: Stomach/gut contents of three randomly selected amphipods collected in either February, April or May 2003. Note the high relative abundance of pennate diatoms in the May samples. All pictures taken at 400x magnification.

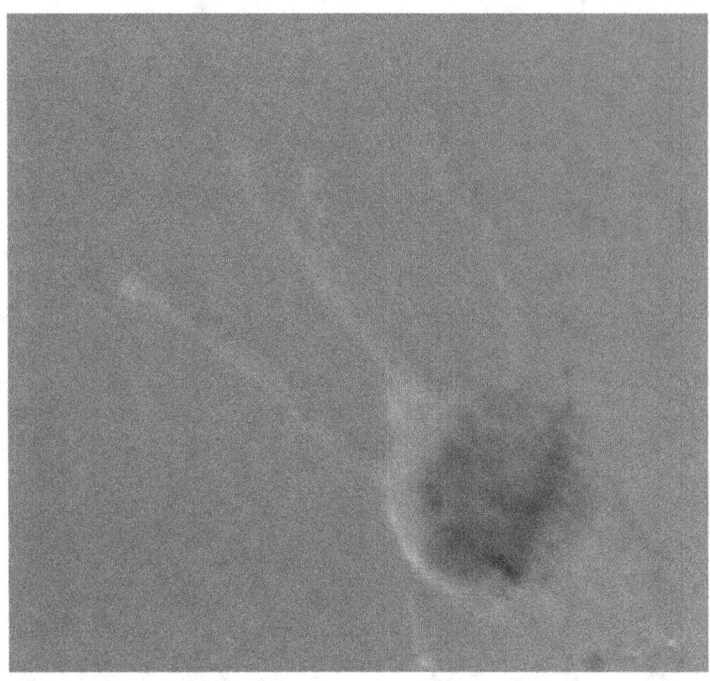

Figure 13: Microphotograph of cnidarian observed in sea ice at site 1. Picture taken at a magnification of 400x, size of body about 70μm.

Discussion

Our study demonstrates that sediment within the ice has a pronounced impact on the seasonal development of the sea ice biota. In the region of high sediment load, the biological development of the spring algal bloom was suppressed, and abundance of sea ice fauna was greatly reduced compared to a clean ice location.

Seasonal development of ice biota through a spring bloom cycle at a clean ice site
Seasonal development of the sea ice primary producers

With increasing day length and, hence, increasing incident light intensity and temperatures in both fast and pack ice, ice algae develop a spring bloom in the bottom cm of the sea ice (Horner & Schrader 1982, Horner 1985, Welch & Bergmann 1989, Gradinger et al. 1991, Welch et al. 1991, Haecky & Andersson 1999, this study).

Within the fast ice, spring ice algal blooms, dominated by diatoms, occur within a time window defined by available light intensity (start) and the seasonal ice melt (end). In general, the timing and the amplitude of ice algal spring bloom (in terms of Chl *a*) observed at our clean ice site 1 followed the pattern observed in earlier Alaskan fast-ice studies (Alexander 1974, Horner & Schrader 1982). With progressing season, under-ice PAR intensities increased from 1.5 μmol photons m^{-2} s^{-1} in February to 7.7 μmol photons

m^{-2} s^{-1} in late May. Ice algae, in general, are adapted to low-light conditions (Cota & Smith 1991, Cota et al. 1991, Kirst & Wiencke 1995, Mock & Gradinger 1999), and the onset of ice algal spring bloom formation in the field occurs after PAR exceeds threshold values of about 2 μmol photons m^{-2} s^{-1} (Horner & Schrader 1982). Thus, light alone has a sufficiently large limiting effect to explain the low concentrations of algae in February 2003, when light intensities were just approaching the threshold for ice algal primary production. PAR values exceeded the threshold later in the season, which coincided with the observed biomass increase.

Besides light, temperature has a major impact on ice algal growth. Firstly, low ice temperatures, down to -25°C at the surface of Barrow fast ice in February 2003, directly reduce physiological process rates. One of the very few studies on temperature effects on ice biota revealed Q_{10} values of about 1 to 5 for Antarctic ice algae (Kottmeier & Sullivan 1988). Secondly, low temperatures result in high brine salinities and, therefore, osmotic stress for sympagic biota (Kirst & Wiencke 1995, Gradinger 2002). The salinity within the brine channel network of ice algae is a direct function of the ice temperature; for example, salinities above 100 ppt occur at temperatures below -6°C (Assur 1958). Experimental studies with cultures of Arctic and Antarctic ice algae showed slower or completely inhibited growth with decreasing temperatures and increasing salinity (Grant & Horner 1976, Zhang et al. 1999, Arrigo 2003). We measured such low temperatures (and consequently high brine salinities) in the upper parts of the ice cores taken in February and April (Fig. 2). The relatively warm and constant temperatures in less than 10cm distance from the bottom of the sea ice (above -2°C in April and May) put – at that time of the year – no thermal and salinity restrictions on the formation of ice-bottom community, which contributed 93% to the total integrated algal pigment content in April 2003 at site 1. In addition to light and temperature, limited supply of nutrients from the water column into the ice restricts high algal biomass accumulation to the bottom cm of the ice/water interface region (e.g., Cota et al. 1987). The strong increase in algal pigment concentration within the lowermost decimeter of the fast ice at site 1 (Fig. 5) can be explained by constant nutrient advection from the water into the ice which allows for favorable growth conditions (and in the end elevated biomass values) closest to the ice-water interface. We doubt that differences in nutrient availability between site 1 and site 2 caused the differences that we observed between ice algal biomass at the sites in 2003, as the control data from April 2002 revealed high algal abundances and biomass values at both sites Similar to earlier investigations, the ice algal bloom community was dominated by diatoms; we did not observe any indications of blooms by freshwater algae as Melnikov et al. (2001) found during the pack ice observations of the SHEBA study.

We conclude that the combination of seasonally varying gradients of light, temperature and nutrient availability led to a bottom ice algal bloom in the spring (Fig. 4) that, in April 2003, resulted in 20-fold higher algal biomass than in February. The observed temporal increase in Chl a is in the same range as the published factors of about 10-fold for algal and bacterial biomass in comparable studies (Horner 1980, Smith et al. 1988, Gradinger et al. 1991, Haecky & Andersson 1999). By April 2003, the integrated algal biomass at site 1 (8.3 mg Chl a m^{-2} for total ice thickness) was higher than in pack ice of the transpolar drift system in the spring (Gradinger 1999a and unpublished data;

median = 1.4 mg Chl a m^{-2}), but lower than in other Arctic near-shore studies, where maximum values exceeded 300 mg Chl *a* m^{-2} (Smith et al. 1990). By the end of May 2003, a total POC concentration of 15.2 ± 1.9 mg C l^{-1} was reached within the bottom 10 cm of the ice core. This value converts to about 1.5 g C m^{-2} and represents the net biomass accumulation over the entire spring bloom. This accumulation is in the same order of magnitude as yearly primary production estimates for fast ice off Barrow (5 g C m^{-2}; Alexander 1974, Horner 1984) and off Narwhal Island (coastal Beaufort Sea, 0.7 g C m^{-2}, Horner & Schrader 1982).

The chlorophyll increase over the 103 days between the February and May sampling converts into an algal growth rate of 0.037 d^{-1}, or an algal doubling time of 18.8 d, assuming that loss terms such as grazing or sedimentation are minor during the build up of the ice algal spring bloom (Gradinger 1999b, Nozais et al. 2001, Michel et al. 2002). This estimate is in accordance with data from other field studies on Arctic (Gradinger et al. 1991: 10 d) and Antarctic pack ice (Grossi et al. 1987: 10 d) under natural snow-cover conditions. All field data, however, are well below the empirical potential growth rate maximum of 0.92 d^{-1} for a temperature of -2°C (Eppley 1972), indicating ignored substantial loss terms, or, more likely, periodically sub-optimal growth conditions (e.g. light limitation) under *in-situ* conditions.

Small-scale spatial patchiness (<2 m) was assessed based on the variability (SD/mean = 9 to 23%) of the Chl *a* concentrations between the four replicates at each sampling date. The results agree with other studies that found small-scale patchiness of <15% in comparable environmental settings, especially similar snow thicknesses. In contrast, larger scale variability on scales of hundreds of meters to hundreds of kilometers between stations in a geographical area can exceed 50% in the same season (Gosselin et al. 1997, Gradinger 1999a, Haecky & Andersson 1999). Again, a significant fraction of these spatial and the above discussed temporal variabilities are related to environmental variables, in particular light availability and nutrient supply modulated by the snow cover, ice morphology and microstructure (Sullivan et al. 1985, Gosselin et al. 1986, Cota & Horne 1989, Eicken et al. 1991, Gradinger et al. 1991, Legendre et al. 1991).

Seasonal development of sea ice fauna

Total ice meiofauna abundance increased, with increasing algal biomass, from 17,600 Ind m^{-2} in February to 276,210 Ind m^{-2} in late May at site 1. At site 1, polychaetes dominated in April. Later in spring, polychaete abundance decreased and nematodes were the dominant taxa. At site 2, nematode abundance decreased from February to May, while polychaetes increased slowly to a maximum of 5900 Ind m^{-2}. Copepods (mainly harpacticoids and cyclopoids) and their nauplii, turbellarians, nematodes and polychaete juveniles formed the dominant metazoan ice meiofauna taxa. These findings are similar to observations from other near-shore Arctic studies with respect to seasonality and relative composition (e.g. Cross, 1982, Kern & Carey 1983, Carey 1985, Grainger & Hsiao 1990, Nozais et al. 2001, Michel et al. 2002). Ciliates, which can numerically dominate the sea ice fauna >20μm (Gradinger et al. 1991, Gradinger 1999b, Nozais et al. 2001) were observed regularly, but were not quantitatively documented. The ice meiofauna composition closely resembles that of the Arctic benthic meio- and macrofauna in near-shore waters (this study, Carey & Montagna 1982, Feder & Schamel 1976, Szymelfenig et al. 1995, Schizas and Shirley 1996); the linkage between sea ice and benthic realm is discussed below. The dramatic changes in Arctic sea ice meiofauna composition, specifically the lack of nematodes, as observed in offshore pack ice, and suggested to be related to climate change (Melnikov et al. 2001), were not detected in our study.

In terms of taxononomic composition, we made one unusual find: the first record of Cnidaria (Fig. 13) as a regular component of the sympagic fauna. This taxon was observed in abundances of 40 to 1500 individuals m^{-2} in the live counts and occurred throughout the study period. We observed mainly very small medusae (approximately 1mm), which were gliding slowly along the bottom of the counting chamber. Polyps were larger, but rare. We assume that previous studies have overlooked the cnidarians due to their transparent nature, their small size and the negative effects of direct ice melt and/or fixation, similar to the case of ciliates (e.g., Gradinger 1999b). A benthic origin, common for other coastal fast-ice meiofauna taxa (Carey 1985) is also likely for these cnidarians.

The immigration of meroplanktic larvae of benthic copepods, polychaetes and gastropods into Arctic sea ice has previously been reported for near-shore Chukchi and Beaufort waters (Carey & Montagna 1982, Cross 1982, Kern & Carey 1983, Nozais et al. 2001). In this study, the major immigration of larval and juvenile polychaetes into the sea ice occurred between February (40 individuals m^{-2}) and April (137,000 individuals m^{-2}). Food availability, mainly ice algae, is likely the major reason for the increase in polychaete numbers, as herbivory appears to be the dominant feeding strategy for ice meiofauna in general (Grainger & Hsiao 1990). The observed dominance of diatoms (Fig. 7) at site 1 provided a favorable food source for meiofauna (Grainger & Hsiao 1990) at site 1, which was not available for meiofauna in the ice at site 2 or for zooplankton at either site during our study period. At the time of the polychaete abundance maximum in the ice, the Chl a concentration of the ice bottom community was 760 times or two orders of magnitude higher than in the water column (see also Alexander 1974, Horner & Schrader 1982). Our data support the hypothesis that polychaete larvae and juveniles use sea ice as a nursery ground (Carey 1992), whereas the adults inhabit the benthos. Polychaete juveniles from our study showed a positive phototactic behavior known from several polychaete species (e.g. McCarthy et al. 2002). This may provide a mechanism for moving from the plankton into the brighter sea ice, a change from a meroplanktic to a lifestyle we define analogously as *merosympagic*. The density decrease of the ice-associated polychaete juveniles between April and late May suggests either active downward migration towards the sea floor or passive release through ice melt, as indicated by the warm ice temperatures in May. The slightly enriched $\delta^{13}C$ values in the seawater (Fig. 3f) and higher Chl a/phaeophytin ratios (Fig. 3d) at the sea floor in May compared to April also point towards a loss of organic matter from the ice into the water column and to the sea floor. On the other hand, polychaete juveniles might have out-grown the brine channel diameters by late May, forcing them out of the sea ice or they changed to negative phototaxis (McCarthy et al. 2002). The brine channel network, with diameters of less than 1mm, sets an upper size limit for its inhabitants (Krembs et al.

2000). Although we did not measure the polychaetes, we observed that the majority of polychaetes were larger by late spring.

Nematodes are another well-documented major component of the Arctic sea ice meiofauna. In coastal areas, several investigators noted this taxon to be especially abundant in late spring/early summer (May–June; Kern & Carey 1983, Grainger et al. 1985, Carey 1992, this study). Very similar to our observations, Carey (1992) observed a seasonal shift in dominance from polychaetes (67% in March) to nematodes later in the season (77% of total abundance in May) in fast ice in Stefansson Sound near Prudhoe Bay. The relatively late increase of nematode abundances could be related to their nutritional ecology: Tschesunov and Riemann (1995) proposed dissolved organic material (DOM), which can reach very high concentrations within the ice matrix (Thomas and Papadimitriou 2003), likely at the end of the bloom, as a potential food source for ice nematodes. In the present study, the increase in nematode abundance was the result of major reproductive activity during May sampling. It remains unclear whether the observed association of the nematode egg cases with microalgal aggregates was an artifact introduced by sampling processing, or whether it reflects a natural preference.

The abundances of sympagic copepod nauplii, copepodites and adult copepods followed the temporal trend of the sympagic polychaetes with peak abundances of 24,300 and 1,370 individuals m^{-2}, respectively, in April 2003. This is contrary to Carey's (1992) finding of a continuous increase in copepod abundance until the end of May. The comparatively high ratio of nauplii can result either from immigration of early nauplii stages into the ice or reproduction of adults within the sea ice. Examples for both strategies are documented: pelagic Antarctic copepods use coastal sea ice as a nursery ground (e.g. Kurbjeweit et al. 1993, Schnack-Schiel 2003), while Arctic and Antarctic harpacticoid sympagic copepods reproduce within the sea ice (Kern & Carey 1983, Carey 1992).

The abundance of zooplankton increased by a factor of 13 from February to May. The total zooplankton abundance remained below max. 24,100 individuals m^{-2} and reached only 10–12% of the abundances of the sea ice meiofauna at site 1. Copepods, by far, dominated the zooplankton with copepodites and adults contributing >90% in February and April and nauplii contributing 69% in May. The predominance of copepods in the epipelagic zones of the Arctic in general is well established (e.g. Smith & Schnack-Schiel 1990, Mumm 1993, Mumm et al. 1998). The seasonal increase in abundance, which is mainly due to an increase in larval stages in May, is reflected in a significant correlation (p <0.01) between zooplankton abundance and surface light, a proxy for progressing season, and coincides with the onset of ice melt. In our study, however, phytoplankton concentrations remained low in late May. For many Arctic copepod species, reproduction (and thus occurrence of nauplii) is not synchronized with the onset of the spring bloom, but is based on storage products (Smith & Schnack-Schiel 1990); the first nauplii stages are typically non-feeding. Ice melt following the end of our study period will lead to increased water column algal concentrations, mainly diatoms, through the increase of light intensities, water column stratification and release of ice algae, and thus improved feeding conditions for later stages of pelagic fauna in the following months (e.g., Horner & Schrader 1982, Smith & Sakshaug 1990).

Impact of sediment load on ice algal biomass

The occurrence of considerable amounts of sediment within sea ice is a well-documented phenomenon in the Arctic in general (e.g. Nürnberg et al. 1994), and in our study area, the Chukchi and Beaufort Seas, in particular (Barnes & Reimnitz 1973, Barnes et al. 1982, Osterkamp & Gosink 1984). Up to 50% of the entire Arctic ice cover can contain visually detectable amounts of sediment (Pfirman et al. 1989, Reimnitz et al. 1993, Nürnberg et al. 1994), which can be transported across the offshore Arctic with the ice drift. Ice gouging and the lifting of anchor ice can lead to incorporation of coarse material. This incorporation can include animal relicts like ostracod or bivalve shells, from the sea floor, in up to about 60 m water depth (Barnes et al. 1984, Reimnitz et al. 1987). Fine-grained sediments are incorporated during frazil ice formation in turbulent conditions and tend to be evenly distributed on a horizontal and vertical scale (Osterkamp & Gosink 1984, Kempema et al. 1989, Reimnitz et al. 1993, Eicken et al. 1997). In the present study, the homogenous distribution of fine-grained sediment in the top 40 cm of the ice cores at site 2 suggests suspension-freezing as the mechanism for sediment incorporation. The total seston (sediment and other particles) content of the sediment-loaded ice at site 2 (102 g DM m^{-2}) was within the range of data reported from visibly discolored ice, "dirty ice", in the Transpolar Drift, and the Laptev and Beaufort Seas (100 to 200 g DM m^{-2}; Reimnitz et al. 1993, Nürnberg et al. 1994, Eicken et al. 1997, Eicken et al. 2000). "Clean ice" has a particle load that is about 20 times lower (6 g DM m^{-2} in this study at site 1, see also references above).

Until now, the role of sediment on the light regime had only been studied from the perspective of ice albedo and attenuation, whereas biological consequences had not been evaluated. High seston concentrations in dirty sea ice have profound impacts on the light regime experienced by the sea ice biota underneath (Osterkamp & Gosink 1984, Light et al. 1998), similar to the shading effect of the snow cover (Maykut 1985, Gradinger et al. 1991). Over the period of time of our observations, available light at the sea ice/water interface at the dirty ice location (site 2) was reduced by 99.8–100% compared to the clean ice site (site 1), and photon flux densities ranged between 0 and 0.5 µmol photons m^{-2} s^{-1}. The spectral attenuation at the clean ice site had a minimum at around 580 to 600 nm, which indicates that the high concentrations of ice algae affected the light spectrum at the clean ice site but not at the dirty ice site, where sediment likely shaped the spectrum (Beeler SooHoo et al. 1987, Light et al. 1998, this study). The shading effect of ice algae also explains the decline in the ratios of transmitted light at site 1 from 4.4% in February to 1.4% in April with increasing algal biomass.

The reduced light availability in the PAR range in dirty sea ice explains the slow algal growth relative to the sediment-free site (for summary of data see Table 4). Even in May, the photon flux densities in the sediment-laden ice were still just approaching the threshold light intensity required for ice algal growth as determined by Mock and Gradinger (1999) in *in-situ* primary production measurements of Arctic pack ice samples. The photon flux density was below levels where biomass build-up was observed in the field (Horner & Schrader 1982). At comparable photon flux density levels of 0.3–0.4 μmol photons $m^{-2} s^{-1}$, no algal growth was observed over 19 days in an artificially darkened Arctic pack ice area (Gradinger et al. 1991). Over the four months of our observations, slow algal growth at an estimated doubling time of 49 days occurred at the dirty ice site; this is 31 days longer or 2.6 times slower than at the clean ice site. We largely exclude site-specific differences other than sediment as a cause for this difference as the snow load was similar at both sites and a rich algal bloom had formed at this site when it was sediment-free in April 2002. The break-up event that occurred in December 2002 at site 1 certainly increased the differences between site 1 and 2, as it resulted in thinner ice at site 1 (0.4m difference in Feb 2003). This thinner ice subsequently allowed for relatively higher light intensities and thus faster algal growth at site 1. However, this effect is minor compared to the sediment impact on the light regime at site 2, where the observed reduction of PAR was equivalent to the combined effect of a 50 cm snow load on 3 m thick sea ice (Maykut 1985). These values exceed by far any observed differences in the physical properties between site 1 and 2. The strong site-to-site variability in sediment load provides an example of the already mentioned larger-scale patchiness of ice properties. The two sites we studied can be seen as two naturally occurring extremes in the spatial patchwork within the Alaskan fast ice zone.

We conclude that the influence of sea ice sediment is as important as snow cover, if not more important, in controlling ice algal growth in Arctic sea ice by modulating the available light intensities. It was not one of our objectives to study the spatial characteristics of the sea ice sediments in our study area. Experiments with graded snow cover (see citation above) had revealed that manipulations of snow cover on scales of 10x10 m are sufficient to alter the light climate and algal growth. We, therefore, assume that the minimum spatial dimension needed for sediment patches to influence ice algal growth is on the order of several meters. The relative contribution of clean to sediment laden fast ice and the variability of sediment load are currently not known and might vary from year-to-year. We recommend that interannual comparisons of algal production incorporate detailed evaluations of the boundary conditions (e.g. light, snow and ice thickness, sediment load throughout the ice column), as year-to-year changes in such boundary conditions will have pronounced impacts on algal growth characteristics.

The reduction of algal growth caused by entrained sediment within sea ice has several broader implications. Previous studies did not sample dirty sea ice but focused primarily on clean ice (e.g. Gosselin et al. 1997, Gradinger 1999a, Gradinger et al. 1999). This suggests an overestimation of Arctic-wide ice algal biomass and primary production estimates as sea ice sediments occur in fast and pack ice in any part of the Arctic, independent of water depth (Nürnberg et al. 1994). While sediment incorporation occurs mainly in water depth less than 30m (see various cited studies of the working groups of Eicken and Reimnitz), the sediment laden sea ice is distributed over the Arctic by the ice drift patterns. Currently, the ice algal primary production in seasonally ice-covered waters is estimated to contribute 4 to 26% to total primary production (Legendre et al. 1992) and above 50% in the permanently ice-covered central Arctic (Gosselin et al. 1997). According to the results of this study, these estimates need to be corrected downward. Based on the observed biomass accumulation in terms of POC, net production in dirty sea ice was reduced to 4% of the clean ice values. Assuming that 40% of the sea ice in the Arctic may be sediment-laden at similar concentrations (Pfirman et al. 1989, Reimnitz et al. 1993, Nürnberg et al. 1994), the impact of dirty ice would lead to a reduction of total annual sea ice primary production by 38%. Global climate change might further enhance the sea ice sediment load and its transport in the Arctic by the increasing frequency and strength of storms and increasing coastal erosion (Proshutinsky et al. 1999, Stierle & Eicken 2002). Anthropogenically generated increase in suspended sediments through coastal and shelf exploration activities may add to this effect and cause further reduction of ice algal productivity on regional to basin-wide scales.

Impact of sediment load on ice meiofauna

Ice meiofauna abundance differed greatly between the two sites in 2003. The observed correlation between meiofauna density and POC and pigment concentrations, respectively, suggests that the ice is primarily used as a habitat in which to feed and may be less important as a habitat *per se*. Both functions have previously been discussed (Carey 1985, Grainger & Hsiao 1990, Krembs et al. 2000, Gradinger 2002, Schnack-Schiel 2003). The relevance as a food-bearing habitat is supported by the differences in absolute densities between the two sites in 2003: few individuals were attracted to dirty ice that provided protection from potential predators, but little food. Again, we consider the location *per se* unlikely as a cause for these differences, even though one could argue that fewer organisms may have been available to recruit to the ice. Ice meiofauna concentrations, however, were very high at site 2 in April 2002 and zooplankton abundance in the water column was similar to that at the clean ice site.

In addition to the limited food availability in dirty ice, the reduced light under the ice may have had an impact on faunal abundance in itself. McCarthy et al. (2002) reported ontogenetic changes in the phototaxis of meroplanktic polychaete larvae. One day old larvae were positively attracted, while older larvae (28 days) responded negatively to light. We propose that the observed positive phototactic behavior of the polychaete juveniles in our study may cause an avoidance of dirty ice patches. Attraction to the brightest spots of sea ice in early spring (February – March) may select for best initial conditions for later algal growth.

Analysis of the ice based food web using stable isotope data

The analysis of stable carbon isotopes provides information on the carbon sources used in a food web (Fry & Sherr 1988). In our case, organic matter produced in the water and in the sea ice comprised the major primary carbon sources throughout the ice-covered period, and these can have distinctly different isotopic signatures. A typical high latitude marine phytoplankton community, depending on location and time of the year, has a $\delta^{13}C$ signature of -27‰ to -25‰ (Hobson & Welch 1992, Iken et al. 2005). Ice algae have been found to be generally isotopically heavier (=more enriched) than phytoplankton reflected in less negative $\delta^{13}C$ ratios (Hobson et al. 1995, Naidu et al. 2000, Schubert & Calvert 2001). As a mechanism, restricted CO_2 supply into the ice is suggested to cause CO_2 limitation and, consequently, isotopic enrichment (Kennedy et al. 2002, Thomas & Papadimitriou 2003). Our data reflect the wide range of possible $\delta^{13}C$

ratios in ice algae, from -24.9 ± 1.6 ‰ in February to -15.5 ± 0.8 ‰ in late May. This change is, therefore, not caused by any food web interactions but by the growth conditions that ice algae experience in their unique environment. While the February ice algal signatures were close to those of Arctic phytoplankton (this study, Hobson et al. 1995, Schubert & Calvert 2001), the signatures became significantly enriched with increasing POC concentration in the ice. The water column POM $\delta^{13}C$ ratios, in contrast, showed little enrichment over the time of our study. The degree of similarity between ice algal and phytoplankton signatures may be an indicator for the successional state of an ice algal bloom. The previously unappreciated dynamic nature of natural $\delta^{13}C$ ice algal signatures stresses the need to apply them with caution in food web studies (Hobson et al. 1995), because the values may vary greatly depending on the state and magnitude of the algal bloom at the time of release of this food source to the pelagic and benthic realms. Our unprecedented findings demonstrate that it is imperative for field studies to identify the isotopic signatures of the end members (primary producers) of a particular food web for that particular study region and time. The not uncommon approach of choosing one single value for such an end member for a whole study and large region appears to be justifiable for phytoplankton only (if at all), where seasonal changes may be minor. In the case of sea ice, the profound changes in the $\delta^{13}C$ ratios caused by CO_2 limitation suggest that the use of one single number to characterize the isotopic composition of sea ice algae is not justified. In contrast, the entire range of observed data needs to be considered when developing a food web model for a particular region.

Stable isotope ratios show a stepwise enrichment between trophic levels of about 1‰ for $\delta^{13}C$ (DeNiro & Epstein 1981, Hobson & Welch 1992, Post 2002) assuming balanced steady-state conditions, thus allowing identification of relative trophic positions among members of a food web. Our study is the first to generate any stable isotopic data on sea ice meiofauna and to document the changes of isotopic ratios in sea ice meiofauna and sympagic amphipods in relation to their food. A shortcoming of the stable isotope approach for ice meiofauna applications is the high number of small-sized animals required for one single sample, which consequently restricted our observations of stable isotope ratios mainly to site 1 where faunal abundances were sufficiently high for collections. Despite this limitation, the correlation between the increasingly enriched ice particulate organic matter and the meiofauna values at site 1 (Fig. 11) provides further strong evidence for the dominance of herbivory in ice metazoans as suggested by Grainger and Hsiao (1990). These data also support the notion of sea ice as a nursery ground for larvae and juveniles of pelagic and benthic biota as their stable isotope ratios changed synchronously with ice particulate matter. This is substantiated by the few observations from site 2: At site 2, isotopic ratios of the sea ice derived POC remained nearly constant and, consequently, no increase in the ratios of the meiofauna were found (Fig. 11). The scarce fauna that was present in the dirt sea ice at site 2 apparently still fed upon the scarce ice algae. Those, however, were not CO_2 limited enough to have to select the heavy carbon isotope; ice algae and ice fauna at site 2, therefore, remained isotopically depleted relative to the algae and fauna at site 1.

Only in some cases did we observe the expected trophic level difference of about 1‰ for $\delta^{13}C$ in the ice meiofauna values at site 1 relative to the ice POC data for the same time period. This inconsistency is likely due the relatively slow and probably taxon-

34

dependent turnover of newly ingested carbon in the body tissue, which will cause the isotopic ratio of animals (both herbivores and carnivores) to lag behind the changing isotopic signature of the ice particulate organic carbon. These previously unappreciated complexities of the matter necessitate a detailed analysis of body turn-over rates for the dominant ice inhabiting taxa (e.g. amphipods, polychaetes, nematodes) to fully resolve relative contributions of different end members for the nutrition of a particular taxon at a given time of the year.

The lack of isotopic enrichment in the ice associated amphipods from February 2003 to April 2003, when ice algae got progressively enriched, may support Carey and Boudrias's (1987) observation from stomach contents analysis that the amphipod *O. litoralis* utilized ice algae when abundant, while also feeding on other prey at other times. This is in accordance with our own observations. Less fresh material consumed earlier in the season (e.g. detritus, carcasses) has a more enriched $\delta^{13}C$ signature. Ice algae appear to be a more important food source for the amphipods later in the season (May/June) when increased ice porosity and release of material from the ice makes the ice-produced organic matter accessible for larger animals like the amphipods.

The broader role of sea ice in the Arctic marine food web: an integrative summary and outlook

The coastal fast ice biota is fueled by ice algae that accumulate considerable amounts of biomass with seasonally increasing light intensities. The overall contribution of ice algae appears to be small in annually ice covered areas compared to its higher contribution in multi-year ice regimes (4 to 26% versus >50% of total primary production; Legendre et al. 1992). Several studies, however, emphasized the relevance of ice algal production for the growth and survival of sea ice associated, pelagic and benthic animals as the first source of freshly produced organic material after the polar winter (Carey & Boudrias 1987, Carey 1992, Runge et al. 1991, this study). We measured substantial accumulation of algal biomass in sediment-free sea ice between February and May, resulting in a net primary production of 1.5g C m^{-2} over the spring period until end of May. Our stable isotope data revealed that the ice algal biomass is consumed by ice fauna (turbellarians, polychaetes and others). Gut content analyses showed that under-ice amphipods feed mainly on ice diatoms in May.

The role of sea ice for merosympagic biota

The high biomass within the ice is only available to taxa small enough to enter the brine channel network, such as merosympagic larvae of polychaetes, gastropods and crustaceans. This community enters the ice realm for short time periods to graze on the ice algae, mainly diatoms before they return to the benthic and pelagic realms either after ice melt or when their body size exceeds that of the typical dimensions of the brine channels (<1mm in diameter). To what extent these merosympagic forms *depend* on the early availability of high food concentrations in the spring remains to be resolved in experimental studies. Such studies should include investigations on the quality and quantity of the food, changes in the food composition (e.g. from diatoms to flagellates with different sizes) and its effect on growth rates. Inappropriate food concentrations might lead to reproduction failure of the polychaetes and gastropods. Earlier ice melt, an ongoing Arctic warming consequence, together with low phytoplankton concentration, dominated by small flagellates, might lead to such a situation. Our current observations in the coastal Beaufort Sea show that polychaete larvae and juveniles clearly have a preference for the high biomass, diatom dominated sea ice situation that occurs from early April to late May.

The dominance of polychaetes in soft sediment ecosystems of coastal areas, shelf seas and the deep-sea worldwide is well documented (Gage & Tyler 1991, Flach & Heip 1996, Paterson et al. 1998, Glover et al. 2001). This also holds true for Arctic shelf and deep-sea soft sediments (Feder & Schamel 1976, Carey & Ruff 1977, Grebmeier et al. 1988, Kröncke 1994, Bluhm et al. 2005) and is, in part, a consequence of the diverse feeding habits of polychaetes, which allow them to exploit available resources very efficiently (Iken et al. 2005). The majority of benthic polychaete species have a planktonic larval stage, defined as so-called meroplankton. Experiments in non-polar marine environments revealed that (i) survival, growth and development of larval polychaetes can be correlated with phytoplankton concentrations (Qian & Chia 1990), (ii) planktotrophic polychaete larvae may be food limited at times (Hansen 1999), (iii) size of the food items matter (Hansen 1999), and that (iv) larval polychaetes are strongly associated with high food concentrations, specifically marine snow (Shanks & del Carmen 1997). These four observations are applicable to the nearshore Alaskan environment, where only sea ice provides high concentrations of food for herbivorous polychaete larvae and juveniles in the time period from April to the beginning of June. Polychaetes are ecologically important components of benthic communities with respect to, for instance, bioturbation (Hutchings 1998) and as prey for various fish and crab species. In the Arctic, several fishes such as sculpins and eel pouts as well as vertebrates, such as fulmars and walrus, rely on polychaetes for part of their energy supply (Lydersen et al. 1989, Fisher and Stewart 1997, Green et al. 1997, Chiperzak et al. 2003). Thus, variability in the reproductive success of polychaetes and potentially other taxa, using sea ice as a nursery ground, has the potential to impact higher trophic levels.

Our results also show that the sea ice meiofauna followed a certain succession pattern driven by a) reproduction of animals within the ice in the case of nematodes and b) migration into and out of the ice in the case of meroplanktic larvae. These processes lead to distinct changes in the relative composition of the sea ice meiofauna over the course of the spring bloom prior to the ice melt. In contrast to Melnikov et al. (2001), we did not find any evidence for major species changes in both algal and meiofauna taxa relative to earlier studies (see citations above).

The role of sea ice for under-ice biota

Amphipods are the best studied consumers of ice algal production at the ice-water interface in all parts of the Arctic (e.g. Poltermann 2000, Werner and Gradinger 2002, Gradinger and Bluhm 2004). Several species of amphipods are endemic to the multi-year sea ice cover and exploit the ice cover year-round, while benthic species like *Onisimus litoralis* are common in nearshore seasonal ice regimes. We observed substantial ingestion of ice algae by the amphipod *Onisimus litoralis* in May 2003 at site 1 in accordance with Carey and Boudrias (1987). Amphipods in general are an important food for Arctic birds and, maybe most important, for Arctic cod (*Boreogadus saida*). This fish species is frequently observed in close association with fast ice and pack ice year-round, and appears to use the ice both for protection against potential predators and as a feeding

36

habitat, ingesting under-amphipods and zooplankton (e.g. Gradinger and Bluhm 2004 and references therein). Arctic cod, major prey for seals and birds, plays a major role in the entire Arctic marine food web as major link from ice related primary production to birds, seals and finally polar bears. In recent years, the Arctic ice cover has been shrinking and thinning with minimum ice coverage in the Beaufort and Chukchi Seas in 2002–2004 (Serreze et al. 2003, Stroeve et al. 2005). The impact of such changes in the duration and characteristics of the ice cover on the biology in near-shore fast ice and off-shore pack ice regimes has been identified from various Arctic regions including altered primary production patterns, changes in species composition and alterations in the food web structure (e.g. Stirling & Derocher 1993, Gradinger 1995, Melnikov et al. 2001).

Sediment in sea ice

Sediment load in nearshore fast ice changes with time and location due to various naturally occurring processes. Studies over the last 30 years showed that suspension freezing, as a main physical process, causes varying incorporation rates of sediments into the growing ice sheets (Reimnitz et al. 1987) causing year-to-year variability in the location and the extent of sediment incorporation in the sea ice. In near-shore regions, the potential increase of sediment load due to increased coastal erosion (Stierle and Eicken 2002) and various human activities can additionally modify the sediment input. In any case, sediment in sea ice plays a pivotal role in controlling these biological processes in the sea ice in that "dirty fast ice" is drastically slowing the build-up of the ice algal biomass. In our case study, algal doubling times were increased by a factor of 2.6 in dirty sea ice relative to clean sea ice. The reduced light intensities caused a domino effect along the sympagic food chain starting with reducing the build-up of ice algal biomass, followed by diminished development of ice meiofauna densities. We did not observe a notable increase in the abundance of primary producers in dirty ice with increasing light intensities, i.e. no algal group was able to efficiently grow at the very low available light intensities. This finding is consistent with many other observations in the Arctic and Antarctic. The reduced biomass accumulation of primary producers, moreover, altered the cryo-pelagic-benthic coupling processes in two ways: The input of organic matter from the sea ice to the realms below was reduced and the sediment laden ice provided less food for the merosympagic and meroplanktic larvae and juveniles. Future studies should focus on providing regional estimates of light availability at the bottom of the ice (e.g. by ROV, AUV or divers) together with field sampling identifying the role of ice, snow, ice algae and ice sediment in the attenuation of light. Such a study would provide the basis for a reasonably accurate estimate of the impact of sea ice sediment load on the primary production in the Chukchi and Beaufort Seas. Our case study clearly exemplifies the significance of the previously ignored parameter sediment for sea ice biological processes.

Acknowledgements

We wish to thank Barrow Arctic Science consortium for the excellent logistical support during our stays in Barrow in 2002 and 2003. Hajo Eicken, Geophysical Institute at the University of Alaska Fairbanks (UAF), and Peter McRoy and Alan Springer, Institute of Marine Science (IMS) at UAF, were very helpful in providing sampling equipment. Thanks are due to Sang Lee, IMS, Klaus Meiners, Yale University, and Kate

Wedemeyer, Minerals Management Service Anchorage, for assistance during field sampling. Tim Howe and Norma Haubenstock ran the stable isotope samples at the Alaska Stable Isotope Facility, UAF. This project was funded through a research grant from the Coastal Marine Institute (CMI Task Order 85242) and by the School of Fisheries and Oceans Sciences, UAF.

Table 1: Spearman rank correlation matrix (r_s) for the entire sea ice data set based on mean values of each parameter for each sampling date. Significant relationships in bold (p-level <0.05[*]). Light 4π (%) is the ratio of the PAR level at the ice-water interface compared to the surface 2π reading.

	Chl a (μg l^{-1})	Meiofauna abundance (Ind m^{-2})	POC (μg l^{-1})	C/N	Light 4π (%)	Light 2π (μmol photons m^{-2} s^{-1})
Meiofauna abundance (Ind m^{-2})	**.851**[*]					
POC (μg l^{-1})	**.810**[*]	**.929**[*]				
C/N	-.571	-.750	-.643			
Light 4π (%)	.571	-.595	-.524	-.393		
Light 2π (μmol photons m^{-2} s^{-1})	.476	.119	.048	-.250	-.238	
δ^{13}C (‰)	**.905**[*]	.810	**.833**[*]	-.607	-.452	.357

Table 2: δ^{13}C isotopic signatures for sea ice meiofauna and zooplankton from sampling sites 1 (sediment-free sea ice) and 2 (sediment-laden sea ice) for 2002 and 2003. a) Mean δ^{13}C values (‰) for n=2 to n=9 and individual δ^{13}C values for n=1. b) Standard deviations (‰) for n≥3 only. The species/taxa are sorted in taxonomic order. No samples were taken at site 2 in May 2002. Note that site 2 had clean ice in 2002 and dirty ice in 2003. POM=particulate organic matter.

A

Site/Realm	Site 1: sea ice					Site 2: sea ice				Site 1: water column					Site 2: water column			
Date	Apr 02	May 02	Feb 03	Apr 03	May 03	Apr 02	Feb 03	Apr 03	May 03	Apr 02	May 02	Feb 03	Apr 03	May 03	Apr 02	Feb 03	Apr 03	May 03
Taxon																		
POM	-20.42	-13.39	-24.92	-23.83	-15.52	-21.50	-25.54	-25.83	-24.17	-25.95	-24.24	-24.69	-27.14	-24.30	-24.53	-24.90	-28.30	-22.49
Planula											-21.82							
Ctenophora											-21.36							
Turbellaria	-19.30	-17.08		-21.40	-15.36			-20.16			-16.86					-23.76		
Rotifers					-21.95								-22.98					
Nematoda		-16.85	-23.25		-15.63													-19.35
Polychaeta	-22.17	-16.20		-22.73			-22.31		-19.59		-18.02		-23.36			-21.42	-22.64	
Trochophora				-25.19							-20.08	-21.77						
Nauplii								-23.21		-24.05	-20.37		-25.61			-24.60		-22.55
Calanoidea								-24.32		-22.11	-21.19	-23.57	-25.21		-21.83	-22.81	-24.12	-22.06
Calanus glacialis	-22.58									-24.71					-23.42			
Harpacticoidea											-17.01	-20.47	-22.87		-23.20		-22.96	-22.22
Cyclopoidea				-24.15						-21.65	-19.77		-21.37			-23.62		-22.17
Onisimus litoralis			-19.34	-22.02														
Gammaracanthus loricatus			-19.24	-20.40														
Chaetognatha											-21.27							-19.70

B

Site/Realm	Site 1: sea ice					Site 2: sea ice				Site 1: water column					Site 2: water column			
Date	Apr 02	May 02	Feb 03	Apr 03	May 03	Apr 02	Feb 03	Apr 03	May 03	Apr 02	May 02	Feb 03	Apr 03	May 03	Apr 02	Feb 03	Apr 03	May 03
Taxon																		
POM	0.20	2.15	1.64	0.95	0.76	0.11	0.44	0.19	0.15	3.79	0.17	1.85	1.24	2.72	0.15	0.27	1.73	1.15
Turbellaria				1.44	0.38													
Nematoda				0.66	0.62													
Polychaeta											0.33		1.09	0.76				
Naupli																		0.65
Calanoidea										2.02	1.06		2.88	0.46	0.13		1.22	0.45
Calanus glacialis											0.21				0.94			
Harpacticoidea													1.44				2.31	
Cyclopoidea																		
Onisimus litoralis			1.78	1.42														
Gammaracanthus loricatus			0.97	0.47														

Table 3: δ^{15}N isotopic signatures for sea ice meiofauna and zooplankton from sampling at sites 1 (sediment-free sea ice) and 2 (sediment-laden sea ice) for 2002 and 2003. a) Mean δ^{15}N values (‰) for n=2 to n=9 and individual δ^{15}N values for n=1. b) Standard deviations (‰) for n≥3 only. The species/taxa are sorted in taxonomic order. No samples were taken at site 2 in May 2002. Note that site 2 had clean ice in 2002 and dirty ice in 2003. POM=particulate organic matter. This table contains fewer data than table 1 since some samples had sufficient mass for δ^{13}C measurements, but not for δ^{15}N measurements.

A

Site/Realm	Site 1 sea ice					Site 2 sea ice				Site 1 water column					Site 2 water column			
Date	Apr 02	May 02	Feb 03	Apr 03	May 03	Apr 02	Feb 03	Apr 03	May 03	Apr 02	May 02	Feb 03	Apr 03	May 03	Apr 02	Feb 03	Apr 03	May 03
POM	7.74	7.52	6.34	7.90	10.07	8.43	5.61		11.90	10.19	5.92	8.07		15.14	7.28	6.96		13.60
Planula											11.50							
Ctenophora											12.96							
Turbellaria		8.50		9.69														
Rotifers					9.13													
Nematoda		6.00	12.00				11.66											
Polychaeta	7.74	5.71		13.89			8.24	8.49	10.27		7.44		14.63	10.44		10.37	14.68	
Trochophora											11.22	11.39						
Ostracoda													13.97					
Nauplii				10.70			9.62		14.04	10.04	10.48			15.42		8.81		14.11
Calanoidea										12.95		12.56	10.45	15.47	13.61	13.26	11.29	13.85
Calanus glacialis													11.40		11.87		10.86	
Harpacticoidea	7.60										7.39	9.95			9.50		13.67	11.81
Cyclopoidea				11.84			10.58			10.88	10.57					12.06		
Onisimus litoralis			12.90	12.73														
Gammaracanthus loricatus			12.59	11.34														
Chaetognatha											14.44							15.42
Copepoda	9.93								9.18									

B

Site/Realm	Site 1 sea ice					Site 2 sea ice				Site 1 water column					Site 2 water column			
Date	Apr 02	May 02	Feb 03	Apr 03	May 03	Apr 02	Feb 03	Apr 03	May 03	Apr 02	May 02	Feb 03	Apr 03	May 03	Apr 02	Feb 03	Apr 03	May 03
POM	0.38	1.03	1.73	0.65	0.56	0.41	0.61		1.89	0.98	0.39	1.30		0.43	0.92	0.80		0.91
Turbellaria				0.78														
Nematoda					1.54													
Polychaeta				2.03			2.03	1.92			1.14							
Trochophora											0.89							
Nauplii														1.90				0.41
Calanoidea													0.77	0.78	0.48		0.17	
Calanus glacialis													1.62		0.91		0.57	
Harpacticoidea											0.91							
Cyclopoidea											0.34							
Onisimus litoralis			1.24	0.54														
Gammaracanthus loricatus			1.73	0.95														

Table 4: Summary of key findings (mean values or range) regarding the differences in the development of biota in the sea ice, water and at the sea floor in relation to sea ice sediment load.

	Site 1 Without sediment	Site 2: With sediment
Total Seston (g DM m^{-2})	6.7	102.4
Light (% surface irradiance)	0.01–0.05	0–0.0003
Chl a$_{max}$ (µg Chl *a* l^{-1}) in ice	329.3	8.3
Doubling time (d) of ice algae	18.8	49
POC (g C m^{-2}) in ice (May)	1.5	0.05
Ratio Chl conc. ice/water	370	9
Sea ice meiofauna (May, Ind l^{-1})	276,000	12,000
Abundance ratio for metazoans water/sea ice (May 03)	10%	471%
Sea ice polychaetes, (April 03, Ind l^{-1})	136,600	3,100
Chl a$_{max}$ (µg Chl *a* l^{-1}) in water	0.9	0.9
Chl a$_{max}$ (µg Chl *a* g sediment) in surface sediment	5.2	0.4
Organic carbon sediment (% dry weight)	0.4	1.8
Final POC (g C m^{-3}) in water	0.1	0.1

Study products

Presentations:

R. Gradinger and B.A. Bluhm 2001. Susceptibility of sea ice biota to disturbances in the shallow Beaufort Sea. Phase 1: Biological coupling of sea ice with the pelagic and benthic realms. CMI Annual Review, Fairbanks.

R. Gradinger, M. Nielson, and B. Bluhm 2002. Cryo-benthic coupling in coastal sea ice off Barrow, Alaska–concept and preliminary results. AAAS meeting, Fairbanks.

R. Gradinger and B.A. Bluhm 2002. Cryo-benthic coupling in coastal sea ice off Barrow, Alaska–concept and preliminary. IARC, Fairbanks.

R. Gradinger and B.A. Bluhm 2003. From the shoreline across the Arctic shelves: Biological properties of sea ice ecosystems. SEARCH open science meeting, Seattle.

R. Gradinger and B.A. Bluhm 2003. Susceptibility of sea ice biota to disturbances in the shallow Beaufort Sea. Phase 1: Biological coupling of sea ice with the pelagic and benthic realms. CMI Annual Review, Fairbanks.

B.A. Bluhm and R. Gradinger 2003. Evidence for cryo-benthic coupling in coastal Alaskan waters, based on community and stable isotope (^{13}C, ^{15}N) analysis–preliminary results. Gordon Research Conference, "Polar Science", Ventura.

R. Gradinger and B. Bluhm (M. Nielson, presenter) 2004. Susceptibility of sea ice biota to disturbances in the shallow Beaufort Sea. Phase 1: Biological coupling of sea ice with the pelagic and benthic realms. CMI Annual Review, Fairbanks.

C.P. McRoy, R. Gradinger, A. Springer, B. Bluhm, S. Iverson, S. Budge 2004. Stable carbon isotopes reveal food web shifts due to Arctic sea ice decline. AGU Montreal.

R. Gradinger and B. Bluhm (presenter) 2005. Susceptibility of sea ice biota to disturbances in the shallow Beaufort Sea. Phase 1: Biological coupling of sea ice with the pelagic and benthic realms. CMI Annual Review, Fairbanks.

B.A. Bluhm, R. Gradinger, M.R. Nielson 2005. Biological coupling of sea ice with the pelagic and benthic realms: the effect of sediment in sea ice. ASLO Conference, Salt Lake City. Feb 20–25, 2005.

R. Gradinger and B.A. Bluhm (presenter) 2005. Susceptibility of sea ice biota to disturbance in the shallow Beaufort Sea. Phase 1: Biological coupling of sea ice with pelagic and benthic realms. Minerals Management Service Information Transfer Meeting, Anchorage. Mar 14–16, 2005.

B.A. Bluhm, R.R. Gradinger, and M.R. Nielson 2005. The role of sea ice sediments in the seasonal development of near-shore Arctic fast ice biota of Barrow, Alaska. Gordon Research Conference, Polar Science, Ventura. Mar 13–18.

Public outreach

Gradinger, R. and B. Bluhm, ongoing since 2002. Project related webpage:
   http://www.sfos.uaf.edu/research/seaicebiota/cmi/barrow2002/index.html

Gradinger, R. and B. Bluhm 2003. Hidden Life in the Arctic Sea Ice: From Barrow's
   Shore-Fast Ice to the Central Arctic Ocean. Public lecture, Barrow Alaska Feb 15
   2003.

Bluhm B. and R. Gradinger 2003. Explorations under the Pack-Ice of the Arctic Ocean.
   Public lecture, Barrow Alaska. May 31 2003.

Arctic Sounder 2003. "Ice life" plays major role in ecosystem by Earl Finkler. Featuring
   the CMI project.

Barrow public radio station 2003. "Ice life" plays major role in ecosystem by Earl
   Finkler. Featuring the CMI project.

Student training

Mette Nielson, Graduate student at SFOS – participated in project activities since 2002

Reports and publications

R. Gradinger and B.A. Bluhm 2002. First field trip of new CMI project completed. SFOS
   Newsletter 6.

R. Gradinger and B.A. Bluhm 2003. Susceptibility of sea ice biota to disturbances in the
   shallow Beaufort Sea. Phase 1: Biological coupling of sea ice with the pelagic and
   benthic realms. CMI Annual Report 9: 81–88.

R. Gradinger and B.A. Bluhm 2004. Susceptibility of sea ice biota to disturbances in the
   shallow Beaufort Sea. Phase 1: Biological coupling of sea ice with the pelagic and
   benthic realms. CMI Annual Report No. 10: 70–78.

R. Gradinger, B.A. Bluhm and M.R. Nielson (in revision). The pivotal role of sea ice
   sediments for the seasonal development of near-shore Arctic fast ice biota off Barrow,
   Alaska. Mar. Ecol. Prog. Ser.

References

Alexander V 1974. Primary productivity regimes of the onshore Beaufort Sea, with reference to potential roles of ice biota. Reed JC, Sater JR(eds). The Coast and Shelf of the Beaufort Sea. Arlington, The Arctic Institute of North America. 609–635.

ACIA 2004. Impacts of a Warming Arctic: Arctic Climate Impact Assessment. Cambridge Univ Press.

Arar EJ, Collins GB (1992) in vitro determination of chlorophyll a and phaeophytin a in marine and freshwater by fluorescence. EPA Method 445.0.

Arrigo KR 2003. Primary production in sea ice. Thomas DN, Dieckmann GS (eds) Sea ice: An introduction to its physics, biology, chemistry, and geology. Blackwell, Oxford. 143–183.

Assur A 1958. Composition of sea ice and its tensile strength. Nat Res Council Publ 598: 106–138.

Barnes PW, Reimnitz E 1973. The shore fast ice cover and its influence on the currents and sediments along the coast of Northern Alaska. Transact. American Geophys Union 54: 1108.

Barnes PW, Reimnitz E, Fox D 1982. Ice rafting of fine-grained sediment, a sorting and transport mechanism, Beaufort Sea, Alaska. J Sediment Petrol 52: 493–502.

Barnes PW, Rearic DM, Reimnitz E 1984. Ice gouging characteristics and processes. Barnes PW, Schell DM, Reimnitz E (eds) The Alaskan Beaufort Sea. Academic Press, Orlando. 185–212

Beeler SooHoo JB, Palmisano AC, Kottmeier ST, Lizotte MP, SooHoo SL, Sullivan CW 1987. Spectral light absorption and quantum yield of photosynthesis in sea ice microalgae and a bloom of *Phaeocystis pouchetii* from McMurdo Sound, Antarctic. Mar Ecol Prog Ser 39: 175–189.

Bluhm BA, MacDonald IR, Debenham C, Iken K 2005. Macro- and megabenthic communities in the high Arctic Canada Basin: initial findings. Polar Biol 28: 218–231.

Carey AG Jr 1985. Marine ice fauna: Arctic. IN: Horner, R. (ed) Sea ice biota. 173–190. Boca Raton, CRC Press.

Carey AG Jr 1992. The ice fauna in the shallow southwestern Beaufort Sea, Arctic Ocean. J Mar Syst 3: 225–236.

Carey AG Jr, Boudrias MA 1987. Feeding ecology of *Pseudalibrotus* (=*Onisimus*) *litoralis* Krøyer (Crustacea: Amphipoda) on the Beaufort Sea inner continental shelf. Polar Biol 8: 29–33.

Carey AG Jr, Montagna PA 1982. Arctic sea ice faunal assemblage: First approach to description and source of the underice meiofauna. Mar Ecol Prog Ser 8: 1–8.

Carey AG Jr, Ruff RE 1977. Ecological studies of the benthos in the western Beaufort Sea with special reference to bivalve mollusks. Dunbar MJ (ed) Polar oceans. Arctic Institute of North America, Calgary. 505–530.

Chiperzak DB, Hopky GE, Lawrence MJ, Schmid DF, Reist JD 2003. Larval and post-larval fish data from the Canadian Beaufort Sea shelf, July to September 1986. Can Data Rep Fish Aquat Sci 1120: 1–157.

Conde D, Bonilla S, Aubriot L, de Leon R, Pintos W 1999. Comparison of the areal amount of chlorophyll a of planktonic and attached microalgae in a shallow coastal lagoon. Hydrobiologia 408/409: 285–291.

Cota GF, Horne EPW 1989. Physical control of arctic ice algal production. Mar Ecol Prog Ser 52: 111–121.

Cota GF, Legendre L, Gosselin M, Ingram RG 1991. Ecology of bottom ice algae: I. Environmental controls and variabilty. J. Mar. Syst. 2:257-278 Cota GF, Prinsenberg SJ, Bennett EB, Loder JW, Lewis MR, Anning JL, Watson NHF 1987. Nutrient fluxes during extended blooms of Arctic ice algae. J Geophys Res 92: 1951–1962.

Cota GF, Smith REH 1991. Ecology of bottom ice algae: II. Dynamics, distributions and productivity. J. Mar. Syst. 2: 279–295

Cross WE 1982. Under-ice biota at the Pond Inlet ice edge and in adjacent fast ice areas during spring. Arctic 35: 13–27.

Cross WE 1987. Effects of oil and chemically treated oil on primary productivity of high Arctic ice algae studied in situ. Arctic 40 (suppl.1): 266–276.

DeNiro MJ, Epstein S 1981. Influence of diet on the distribution of nitrogen isotopes in animals. Geochim Cosmochim Acta 45: 341–351.

Eicken H 1992. The role of sea ice in structuring Antarctic ecosystems. Polar Biol 12: 3–13.

Eicken H, Ackley SF, Richter-Menge JA, Lange MA 1991. Is the strength of sea ice related to its chlorophyll content? Polar Biol 11: 347–350.

Eicken H, Reimnitz E, Alexandrov V, Martin T, Kassens H, Viehoff T 1997. Sea-ice processes in the Laptev Sea and their importance for sediment export. Continental Shelf Res 17: 205–233.

Eicken H, Kolatschek J, Freitag J, Lindemann F, Kassens H., Dmitrenko I 2000. Identifying a major source area and constraints on entrainment for basin-scale sediment transport by Arctic sea ice. Geophys Res Lett 27: 1919–1922.

Eicken H, Gradinger R, Graves A, Mahoney A, Rigor I, in press. Sediment transport by sea ice in the Chukchi: importance due to changing ice conditions? Deep-Sea Res in press.

Eppley RW 1972. Temperature and phytoplankton growth in the sea. Fish Bull 70: 1063–1085.

Feder HM, Schamel D 1976. Shallow water benthic fauna of Prudhoe Bay. Assessment of the Arctic Marine Environment: Selected Topics, Chapter 22. Institute of Marine Science, University of Alaska, Fairbanks. 329–359.

Fiala M, Delille D 1999. Annual changes of microalgae biomass in Antarctic sea ice contaminated by crude oil and diesel fuel. Polar Biol 21: 391–396.

Fisher KI, Steward REA 1997. Summer foods of Atlantic walrus, *Odobenus rosmarus rosmarus*, in northern Foxe Basin, Northwest Territories. Can J Zool 75: 1166–1175.

Flach E, Heip C 1996. Verticle distribution of macrozoobenthos within the sediment on the continental slope of the Goban Spur area (NE Atlantic). Mar Ecol Prog Ser 141: 55–66.

Fry B, Sherr EB 1988. δ^{13}C Measurements as indicators of carbon flow in marine and freshwater ecosystems. Rundel PW, JR Ehleringer, KA Nagy (eds) Stable isotopes in ecological research. Springer, New York. 13–47.

Gage JD, Tyler PA 1991. Deep-sea biology: a natural history of organisms at the deep-sea floor. Cambridge University Press, Cambridge.

Glover A, Paterson G, Bett B, Gage J, Sibuet M, Sheader M, Hawkins L 2001. Patterns in polychaete abundance and diversity from the Madeira Abyssal Plain, Northeast Atlantic. Deep-Sea Res I48: 217–236.

Gordon HB, O'Farrell SP 1997. Transient climate change in the CSIRO coupled model with dynamic sea ice. Mon Weather Rev 125: 875–907.

Gosselin M, Legendre L, Therriault JC, Demers S, Rochet M 1986. Physical control of the horizontal patchiness of sea-ice microalgae. Mar Ecol Prog Ser 29: 289–298.

Gosselin M, Levasseur M, Wheeler PA, Horner RA, Booth BC 1997. New measurements of phytoplankton and ice algal production in the Arctic Ocean. Deep-Sea Res 44: 1623–1644.

Gradinger R 1995. Climate change and biological oceanography of the Arctic Ocean. Phil Trans R Soc Lond A 352: 277–286.

Gradinger R 1999a. Vertical fine structure of algal biomass and composition in Arctic pack ice. Mar Biol 133: 745–754.

Gradinger R 1999b. Integrated abundances and biomass of sympagic meiofauna from Arctic and Antarctic pack ice. Polar Biol 22: 169–177.

Gradinger R 2002. Sea ice microorganisms. In: Bitten G (ed) Encyclopedia of Environmental Microbiology. Wiley & Sons, New York. 2833–2844.

Gradinger R, Friedrich C, Spindler M 1999. Abundance, biomass and composition of the sea ice biota of the Greenland Sea pack ice. Deep-Sea Res 46: 1457–1472.

Gradinger R, Ikävalko J 1998. Organism incorporation into newly forming Arctic sea ice in the Greenland Sea. J Plankton Res 20: 571–586.

Gradinger R, Spindler M 1997. Coupled ecosystems in the ice-covered Arctic Ocean. Stel JH, Borst JC, Droppert LJ, vd Meulen J (eds) Operational oceanography. The challenge for European co-operation. Amsterdam, Elsevier Science. 385–390.

Gradinger R, Bluhm BA 2003. Susceptibility of sea ice biota to disturbances in the shallow Beaufort Sea. Phase 1: Biological coupling of sea ice with the pelagic and benthic realms. Univ Alaska Fairbanks, CMI. Annual Rep 9: 81–88.

Gradinger RR, Bluhm BA 2004. *In situ* observations on the distribution and behavior of amphipods and Arctic cod (*Boreogadus saida*) under the sea ice of the high Arctic Canadian Basin. Polar Biol 27: 595–603.

Gradinger R, Spindler M, Henschel D 1991. Development of Arctic sea-ice organisms under graded snow cover. Polar Res 10: 295–307.

Gradinger R, Meiners K, Plumley G, Zhang Q, Bluhm BA 2005. Abundance and composition of the sea ice meiofauna in off-shore pack ice of the Beaufort Gyre in summer 2002 and 2003. Polar Biol 28: 174–181.

Grainger EH, Hsiao SIC 1990. Trophic relationships of the sea ice meiofauna in Frobisher Bay, Arctic Canada. Polar Biol 10: 283–292.

Grainger EH, Mohammed AA, Lovrity JE 1985. The sea ice fauna of Frobisher Bay, Arctic Canada. Arctic 38: 23–30.

Grant WS, Horner RA 1976. Growth responses to salinity variation in four Arctic ice diatoms. J Phycol 12: 180–185.

Grebmeier JM, McRoy CP, Feder HM 1988. Pelagic-benthic coupling on the shelf of the northern Bering and Chukchi Seas. I. Food supply source and benthic biomass. Mar Ecol Prog Ser 48: 57–67.

Green JM, Mitchell LR, Reynolds JB 1997. Biology of the fish doctor, an eel out, from Cornwallis Island, Northwest Territories, Canada. Symp Am Fish Soc 19: 140–147.

Grossi SM, Kottmeier ST, Moe RL, Taylor GT, Sullivan CW 1987. Sea ice microbial communities. VI. Growth and primary production in bottom ice under graded snow cover. Mar Ecol Prog Ser 35: 153–164.

Haecky P, Andersson A 1999. Primary and bacterial production in sea ice in the northern Baltic Sea. Aquat Microb Ecol 20: 107–118.

Hansen BW 1999. Cohort growth of planktotrophic polychaete larvae – are they food limited? Mar Ecol Prog Ser 178: 109–119.

Hobson KA, Welch H 1992. Determination of trophic relationships within a high Arctic marine food web using ∂13C and ∂15N analysis. Mar Ecol Progr Ser 84: 9–18.

Hobson KA, Ambrose WGJ, Renaud PE 1995. Sources of primary production, benthic-pelagic coupling, and trophic relationships within the NE Water Polynya: Insights from ∂13C and ∂15N analysis. Mar Ecol Prog Ser 128: 1–10.

Horner R 1976. Sea ice organisms. Oceanogr Mar Biol Ann Rev 14: 167–182.

Horner R 1980. Ecology and productivity of Arctic sea ice diatoms. Ross R Proc 6th Symp Recent Fossil Diatoms. Königstein, Koeltz. 359–369.

Horner R 1984. Primary productivity of the western Beaufort Sea. Barnes PW, Schell DM, Reimnitz E (eds) The Alaskan Beaufort Sea. Orlando, Academic Press. 295–310.

Horner R 1985. Sea ice biota. CRC press, Boca Raton.

Horner R, Schrader GC 1982. Relative contribution of ice algae, phytoplankton, and benthic microalgae to primary production in nearshore regions of the Beaufort Sea. Arctic 35: 485–503.

Hutchings P 1998. Biodiversity and functioning of polychaetes in benthic sediments. Biodivers Conserv 7: 1133–1145.

Iken K, Bluhm BA, Gradinger R 2005. Food web structure in the high Arctic Canada Basin: evidence from $\partial^{13}C$ and $\partial^{15}N$ analysis. Polar Biol 238–249.

Kempema EW, Reimnitz E, Barnes PW 1989. Sea ice sediment entrainment and rafting in the Arctic. J Sed Pet 59: 308–317.

Kennedy H, Thomas DN, Kattner G, Haas C, Dieckmann GS 2002. Particulate organic carbon in Antarctic summer sea ice: concentration and stable carbon isotopic composition. Mar Ecol Prog Ser 238: 1–13.

Kern JC, Carey AG Jr 1983. The faunal assemblage inhabiting seasonal sea ice in the nearshore Arctic Ocean with emphasis on copepods. Mar Ecol Progr Ser 10: 159–167.

Kirst GO, Wiencke C 1995. Ecophysiology of polar algae. J Phycol 31: 181–199.

Kottmeier ST, Sullivan CW 1988. Sea ice microbial communities (SIMCO). 9. Effects of temperature and salinity on rates of metabolism and growth of autotrophs and heterotrophs. Polar Biol 8: 293–304.

Krembs C, Gradinger R, Spindler M 2000. Implications of brine channel geometry and surface area for the interaction of sympagic organisms in Arctic sea ice. J Exp Mar Biol Ecol 243: 55–80.

Kröncke I 1994. Macrobenthos composition, abundance and biomass in the Arctic Ocean along a transect between Svalbard and the Makarov Basin. Polar Biol 14: 519–529.

Kurbjeweit F, Gradinger R, Weissenberger J 1993. The life cycle of *Stephos longipes* – an example for cryopelagic coupling in the Weddell Sea (Antarctica). Mar Ecol Prog Ser 98: 255–262.

Legendre L, Ackley SF, Dieckmann GS, Gulliksen B, Horner R, Hoshiai T, Melnikov IA, Reeburgh WS, Spindler M, Sullivan CW 1992. Ecology of sea ice biota. 2. Global significance. Polar Biol 12: 429–444.

Legendre L, Aota M, Shirasawa K, Martineau M-J, Ishikawa M 1991. Crystallo-graphic structure of sea ice along a salinity gradient and environmental control of microalgae in the brine cells. J Mar Syst 2: 347–357.

Light B, Eicken H, Maykut GA, Grenfell TC 1998. The effect of included particulates on the spectral albedo of sea ice. J Geophys Res 103: 27739–27752.

Lydersen C, Gjertz I, Weslawski JM 1989. Stomach contents of autumn-feeding marine vertebrates from Hornsund, Svalbard. Polar Rec 25: 107–114.

Macdonald RW 2000. Arctic estuaries and ice: a positive-negative estuarine couple. Lewis EL (ed) The freshwater budget of the Arctic Ocean. Kluwer, Amsterdam. 383–407.

Macdonald RW, Carmack EC, McLaughlin FA, Falkner FK, Swift JH 1999. Connections among ice, runoff and atmospheric forcing in the Beaufort Gyre. Geophys Res Letters 26: 2223–2226.

Maykut GA 1985 The ice environment. Horner R (ed) Sea ice biota. CRC Press, Boca Raton. 21–82.

McCarthy DA, Forward RB, Young CM 2002. Ontogeny of phototaxis and geotaxis during larval development of the sabellariid polychaete *Phragmatopoma lapidosa*. Mar Ecol Prog Ser 241: 215–220.

Melnikov I, Zhitina LS, Kolosova HG 2001. The Arctic sea ice biological communities in recent environmental changes. Mem Natl Inst Polar Res Spec Issue 54: 409–416.

Michel C, Nielsen TG, Nozais C, Gosselin M 2002. Significance of sedimentation and grazing by ice micro- and meiofauna for carbon cycling in annual sea ice (northern Baffin Bay). Aquat Microb Ecol 30: 57–68.

MMS 2001. Liberty Development production plan, draft environmental impact statement. OCS EIS/EA MMS 2001-001. U.S. Department of the Interior, Minerals Management Service, Alaska OCS Region, Anchorage.

Mock T, Gradinger R 1999. Determination of Arctic ice algal production with a new and easy *in situ* incubation technique. Mar Ecol Prog Ser 177: 15–26.

Mumm N 1993. Composition and distribution of mesozooplankton in the Nansen Basin, Arctic Ocean, during summer. Polar Biol 13: 451–461.

Mumm N, Auel H, Hanssen H., Hagen W, Richter C, Hirche H-J 1998. Breaking the ice: large-scale distribution of mesozooplankton after a decade of Arctic and transpolar cruises. Polar Biol 20: 189–197.

Naidu AS, Cooper LW, Finney BP, Macdonald RW, Alexander C, Semiletov IP 2000. Organic carbon isotope ratios ($d^{13}C$) of Arctic Amerasian continental shelf sediments. Int J Earth Sci 89: 522–532.

Nansen F 1897. In Nacht und Eis. Leipzig, Brockhaus.

Nozais C, Gosselin M, Michel C, Tita G 2001. Abundance, biomass, composition and grazing impact of the sea-ice meiofauna in the North Water, northern Baffin Bay. Mar Ecol Prog Ser 217: 235–250.

Nürnberg D, Wollenburg I, Dethleff D, Eicken H, Kassens H, Letzig T, Reimnitz E, Thiede J 1994. Sediments in Arctic sea ice: Implications for entrainment, transport and release. Mar Geol 119: 185–214.

Osterkamp TE, Gosink JP 1984 Observations and analyses of sediment-laden sea ice. In: Barnes PW, Schell DM, Reimnitz E (eds) The Alaskan Beaufort Sea: ecosystems and environments. Academic Press, Orlando, 73–93.

Parkinson CL, Cavalieri DJ, Gloersen P, Zwally HJ, Comiso JC 1999. Arctic sea ice extents, areas, and trends, 1978–1996. J Geophys Res 104: 20837–20856.

Paterson GLJ, Wilson GDF, Cosson N, Lamont PA 1998. Hessler and Jumars (1974) revisited: abyssal polychaete assemblages from the Atlantic and Pacific. Deep-Sea Res 45: 225–251.

Pfirman S, Gascard JC, Wollenburg I, Mudie P, Abelmann A 1989. Particle-laden Eurasian Arctic sea ice: observations from July and August 1987. Polar Res 7: 59–66.

Poltermann M 2000. Growth, production and productivity of the Arctic sympagic amphipod *Gammarus wilkitzkii*. Mar Ecol Prog Ser 193: 109–116.

Post DM 2002. Using stable isotopes to estimate trophic position: Models, methods and assumptions. Ecology 83: 703–718.

Proshutinsky A, Polyakov IV, Johnson MA 1999. Climate states and variability of Arctic ice and water dynamics during 1946–1997. Polar Res 18: 1–8.

Qian P-Y, Chia F-S 1990. Detritus as a potential food source for polychaete larvae. J Exp Mar Biol Ecol 143: 63–71.

Reimnitz E, Kempema EW, Barnes PW 1987. Anchor ice, seabed freezing, and sediment dynamics in shallow arctic seas, J Geophys Res 92: 14671–14678.

Reimnitz E, Marincovich L Jr, McCormick M, Briggs WM 1992. Suspension freezing of bottom sediment and biota in the Northwest Passage and implications for Arctic Ocean sedimentation, Can J Earth Sci 29: 693–703.

Reimnitz E, Barnes PW, Weber WS 1993. Particulate matter in pack ice of the Beaufort Gyre. J Glaciol 39: 186–198.

Rothrock D, Yu Y, Maykut G 1999. The thinning of the Arctic ice cover. Geophys Res Letters 26: 3469–3472.

Runge JA, Therriault J-C, Legendre L, Ingram RG, and Demers S. Coupling between ice microalgal productivity and the pelagic, metazoan food web in southeastern Hudson Bay: a synthesis of results. Polar Rec 10(2), 325–338. 91.

Sakshaug E 1991. Food webs and primary production in the Barents Sea. Proc NIPR Symp Polar Biol 4: 1–8.

Schizas NV, Shirley TC 1996. Seasonal change in structure of an Alaskan intertidal meiofaunal assemblage. Mar Ecol Prog Ser 133: 115–124.

Shanks AL, del Carmen KA 1997. Larval polychaetes are strongly associated with marine snow. Mar Ecol Prog Ser 154: 211–221.

Smith REH, Anning J, Clement P, Cota G 1988. Abundance and production of ice algae in Resolute Passage, Canadian Arctic. Mar Ecol Prog Ser 48: 251–263.

Smith REH, Clement P, Head EJ 1990. Night metabolism of recent photosynthate by sea ice algae in the high Artic. Mar Biol 107: 255–261.

Smith SL, Schnack-Schiel SB 1990. Polar zooplankton. Smith WO Jr (ed) Polar oceanography. Part B. Chemistry, biology, and geology. Academic Press, San Diego. 527–598.

Smith WO Jr, Sakshaug E 1990. Polar phytoplankton. In: Smith, WO Jr Polar oceanography. Part B. Chemistry, biology and geology. 477–525. San Diego, Academic Press.

Schnack-Schiel SB 2003. The macrobiology of sea ice. Thomas DN, Dieckmann GS (eds) Sea Ice: An Introduction to its physics, biology, chemistry, and geology. Blackwell, Oxford. 211–239.

Schubert CJ, Calvert SE 2001. Nitrogen and carbon isotopic composition of marine and terrestrial organic matter in Arctic Ocean sediments: implications for nutrient utilization and organic matter composition. Deep-Sea Res 48: 789–810.

Serreze MC, Maslanik JA, Scambos TA, Fetterer F, Stroeve J, Knowles K, Fowler C, Drobot S, Barry RG, Haran TM 2003. A record minimum arctic sea ice extent and area in 2002. Geophy Res Letters 30:doi:10.1029/2002GL016406.

Stierle AP, Eicken H 2002. Sedimentary inclusions in Alaskan coastal sea ice: small scale distribution, interannual variability and entrainment requirements. Arctic Antarctic Alpine Res 34: 465–476.

Stirling I, Derocher AE 1993. Possible impacts of climatic warming on polar bears. Arctic 46: 240–245.

Stroeve JC, Serreze MC, Fetterer F, Arbetter T, Meier W, Maslanik J, Knowles K 2005. Tracking the Arctic's shrinking ice cover: Another extreme September minimum in 2004. Geophysical Research Letters 32 (4): Art. No. L04501.

Sullivan C W, Palmisano AC, Kottmeier S, McGrath Grossi S, Moe R 1985. The influence of light on growth and development of the sea-ice microbial community in McMurdo Sound. Siegfried WR, Condy PR, Laws RM (eds) Antarctic nutrient cycles and food webs. Berlin, Springer. 78–83.

Szymelfenig M, Kwasniewski S, Weslawski JM 1995. Intertidal zone of Svalbard. 2. Meiobenthos density and occurrence. Polar Biol 15: 137–141.

Thomas DN, Papadimitriou S 2003. Biogeochemistry of sea ice. Thomas DN, Dieckmann GS (eds) Sea ice. An introduction to its physics, chemistry, biology and geology. Blackwell, Oxford. 267–302.

Tschesunov AV, Riemann F 1995. Arctic sea ice nematodes (Monhysteroidea) with descriptions of *Cryonema crassum* gen. n. sp. n. and *C. tenue* sp. n. Nematol 41: 35–50.

Welch HE, Bergmann MA 1989. Seasonal development of ice algae and its prediction from environmental factors near Resolute, N.W.T., Canada. Canadian J Fish Aquatic Sci 46: 1793–1804.

Welch HE, Bergmann MA, Siferd TD, Amarualik PS 1991. Seasonal development of ice algae near Chesterfield Inlet, N.W.T., Canada. Can J Fish Aquatic Sci 48: 2395–2402.

Werner I, Gradinger R 2002. Under-ice amphipods in the Greenland Sea and Fram Strait (Arctic): environmental controls and seasonal patterns below the pack ice. Mar Biol 140: 317–326.

Zhang Q, Gradinger R, Spindler M 1999. Experimental study on the effect of salinity on growth rates of Arctic-sea-ice algae from the Greenland Sea. Boreal Env Res 4: 1–8.

Data appendix I

Table 1: Mean abundances with standard deviations (STDV) of four replicates for phytoplankton and sea ice samples collected at site 1 and/or 2

Location	Date	size classes (ESD)	total number of cells/ml mean	total number of cells/ml STDV
Site 1: Sediment-free ice	2/13/03			
		10	38193	7249
		20	4736	899
		100	941	179
		200	25	5
		1000	0	0
Site 1: Sediment-free ice	5/28/03	size classes (ESD)	total number of cells/ml mean	total number of cells/ml STDV
		10	153312	18355
		20	41323	4947
		100	10725	1284
		200	0	0
		1000	0	0
Site 1:Phytoplankton	2/13/03	size classes (ESD)	total number of cells/ml mean	total number of cells/ml mean
		10	4353	1734
		20	1226	488
		100	262	104
		200	0	0
		1000	0	0
Site 1:Phytoplankton	5/28/03	size classes (ESD)	total number of cells/ml mean	total number of cells/ml mean
		10	10037	3325
		20	1855	614
		100	340	112
		200	28	9
		1000	0	0
Site 2: Sediment-laden ice	2/15/03	size classes (ESD)	total number of cells/ml mean	total number of cells/ml STDV
		10	84438	28036
		20	10964	3640
		100	1200	399
		200	0	0
		1000	0	0
Site 2: Sediment-laden ice	5/30/03	size classes (ESD)	total number of cells/ml mean	total number of cells/ml STDV
		10	150922	31261
		20	44996	9320
		100	2093	433
		200	0	0
		1000	0	0

Site 2: Phytoplankton	2/15/03	size classes (ESD)	total number of cells/ml mean	total number of cells/ml STDV
		10	13630	3136
		20	3163	728
		100	347	80
		200	0	0
		1000	0	0

Site 2: Phytoplankton	5/30/03	size classes (ESD)	total number of cells/ml mean	total number of cells/ml STDV
		10	11225	1534
		20	2871	392
		100	265	36
		200	0	0
		1000	0	0

Table 2: Mean abundance (Ind m^{-2}) with standard deviation (SD) of sea ice meiofauna based on four replicate ice cores

Site 1: Sediment-free ice

Taxon	Apr-02	Feb-03	Apr-03	May-03	SD values	Apr-02	Feb-03	Apr-03	May-03
Copepoda	34078	582	1371	629		6923	608	1272	778
Nauplii	3250	1027	24327	6867		2594	668	12214	3476
Polychaetes	3524	36	136694	12283		3263	71	8985	8845
Trochophora	0	0	0	229		0	0	0	325
Turbellaria	4425	5163	17946	8968		2415	1532	2110	2874
Nematoda	41493	9752	3269	232352		37766	2209	1570	39003
Others	0	1093	1495	14878		0	1322	1410	5685

Site 2: Sediment-laden ice

Taxon	Apr-02	Feb-03	Apr-03	May-03	SD values	Apr-02	Feb-03	Apr-03	May-03
Copepoda	165049	848	576	989		27258	544	1038	1255
Nauplii	15462	3339	784	3880		12689	748	547	3840
Polychaetes	16998	1957	3101	5924		15939	1316	3451	5676
Turbellaria	22003	708	58	299		12413	398	115	209
Nematoda	197227	9112	790	53		179434	3294	639	71
Others	0	627	142	813		0	498	176	703

Table 3: Mean and standard deviation (STDV) of zooplankton abundance (Ind/m²) at site 1 and site 2 based on four replicates each.

Site 1

Taxon	Mean				STDV			
	Apr 02	Feb 03	Apr 03	May 03	Apr 02	Feb 03	Apr 03	May 03
Copepoda	11087	2003	23625	8013	12347	769	6338	2298
Nauplii	2314	104	207	19480	992	132	265	1964
Polychaetes	69	0	138	242	80	0	195	132
Trochophora	207	0	0	35	138	0	0	69
Turbellaria	35	0	35	207	69	0	69	239
Nematoda	207	0	0	138	178	0	0	276
Others	69	35	104	242	80	69	207	207

Site 2

Taxon	Mean				STDV			
	Apr 02	Feb 03	Apr 03	May 03	Apr 02	Feb 03	Apr 03	May 03
Copepoda	15404	4179	4697	9844	5699	534	1996	2825
Nauplii	14195	0	35	44624	3867	0	69	6114
Polychaetes	725	0	0	656	306	0	0	413
Trochophora	2590	207	0	104	1994	178	0	132
Turbellaria	69	0	0	276	138	0	0	298
Nematoda	69	35	0	207	80	69	0	178
Others	829	311	104	587	529	207	132	363

56

Table 4. Light intensity (umol photons m^{-2} s^{-1}) and temperature measurements in the water at site 1 and 2. Light intensities were measured with a surface 2π and a submerged 4π sensor

The 4π under-water sensor values were normalized (light 4π corrected) for fluctuations of the surface 2π reference sensor

		Site 1				Site 2			
Date	Water depth (m)	Temperature (C)	Light 2π	Light 4π	Light 4π, corrected	Temperature (C)	Light 2π	Light 4π	Light 4π, corrected
April 2002	0	-1.9	513.3	82.2	82.2	-1.7	956.4	164.2	164.2
	1	-1.9	500.9	29.8	30.5	-1.8	966.2	80.6	79.8
	2	-1.8	480.7	1.9	2.0	-1.8	930.5	4.6	4.7
	3	-1.8	471.2	1.5	1.7	-1.8	860.1	2.5	2.7
	4	-1.8	457.2	0.9	1.0	-1.8	835.1	1.7	1.9
	5	-1.8	452.2	0.6	0.7	-1.8	765.1	1.1	1.3
	5.6	-1.8	424.2	0.5	0.6				
February 2003	0	-2	31.3	93.7	93.7	-1.6	162.9	3.7	3.7
	1	-1.9	31.0	1.7	1.7	-1.6	164.7	0.0	0.0
	2	-1.6	32.7	1.5	1.4	-1.6	185.8	0.0	0.0
	3	-1.6	34.6	1.3	1.1	-1.8	186.1	0.0	0.0
	4	-1.6	35.7	0.9	0.8	-1.9	186.7	0.0	0.0
	5	-1.5	37.6	0.8	0.6		187.1	0.0	0.0
April 2003	0	-1.7	383.1	191.4	191.4	-2.0	646.2	2.2	2.2
	1	-1.7	384.3	30.4	30.3	-1.9	642.4	0.1	0.1
	2	-1.7	393.5	5.6	5.5	-1.8	640.3	0.0	0.0
	3	-1.7	393.1	4.1	4.0	-1.8	634.5	0.0	0.0
	4	-1.7	397.3	2.6	2.5	-1.8	645.0	0.0	0.0
	5	-1.7	404.9	1.8	1.7	-1.7	640.3	0.0	0.0
May 2003	0	-1.3	666.4	202.2	202.2	-1.4	1696.0	48.7	48.7
	1	-1.6	660.9	108.4	109.3	-1.6	1539.0	1.5	1.7
	2	-1.7	655.2	7.7	7.9	-1.7	1544.0	0.4	0.4
	3	-1.7	653.3	5.7	5.8	-1.7	1548.0	0.3	0.3
	4	-1.7	647.7	4.4	4.6	-1.7	1208.0	0.2	0.2
	5	-1.7	642.2	3.5	3.6	-1.7	1103.0	0.1	0.2

Table 5: Mean and standard deviation (STDV) for chlorophyll concentration, chlorophyll/phaeophytin ratio and %organic matter in sea floor sediment at site 1 and 2.

Chlorophyll (µg/l)

time	Mean Site 1	Mean Site 2	STDV Site 1	STDV Site 2
Feb 03	0.5	0.4	0.6	0.1
April 03	0.2	0.4	0.0	0.1
May 03	1.0	0.3	0.7	0.1

Chlorophyll/phaeophytin ratio

time	Mean Site 1	Mean Site 2	STDV Site 1	STDV Site 2
Feb 03	0.2	0.6	0.1	0.0
April 03	0.2	0.8	0.1	0.0
May 03	0.4	5.2	3.8	0.1

% Organic matter

time	Mean Site 1	Mean Site 2	STDV Site 1	STDV Site 2
Feb 03	1.12	6.86	0.27	1.10
April 03	0.53	5.58	0.07	1.80
May 03	0.37	1.82	N/A	0.58

58

Table 6: Mean and standard deviation (STDV) for chlorophyll, particulate organic carbon (POC), d^{13}C ratio chlorophyll/phaeophytin ratio in sea ice and water column at site 1 and 2 based on four replicates each.

Chlorophyll (μg/l)

	Mean				STDV			
time	Site 1: sediment-free ice	Site 1: water	Site 2: Sediment-laden ice	Site 2: water	Site 1: sediment-free ice	Site 1: water	Site 2: Sediment-laden ice	Site 2: water
April 02	45.2	1.6	246.8	0.4	37.5	0.1	23.5	0.0
Feb 03	7.4	0.0	1.9	0.0	0.7	0.0	0.0	0.0
April 03	71.4	0.1	3.3	0.1	16.1	0.0	11	0.0
May 03	329.3	0.9	8.3	0.9	42.0	0.0	7.0	0.4

Chlorophyll/phaeophytin ratio

	Mean				STDV			
time	Site 1: sediment-free ice	Site 1: water	Site 2: Sediment-laden ice	Site 2: water	Site 1: sediment-free ice	Site 1: water	Site 2: Sediment-laden ice	Site 2: water
April 02	18.3	3.8	5.1	1.7	14.9	0.5	1.0	0.3
Feb 03	13.3	1.2	10.3	1.3	1.7	0.2	4.9	0.2
April 03	3.7	0.8	6.8	0.7	0.7	0.1	2.8	0.1
May 03	6.3	1.7	2.7	1.8	1.3	0.1	0.8	0.6

POC (μg/l)

	Mean					STDV			
time	Site 1: sediment-free ice	Site 1: water	Site 2: Sediment-laden ice	Site 2: water		Site 1: sediment-free ice	Site 1: water	Site 2: Sediment-laden ice	Site 2: water
April 02	7.38	0.15	9.64	0.21	0.00	2.37	0.09	1.81	0.05
Feb 03	1.28	0.17	0.98	0.20	0.00	0.62	0.09	0.22	0.05
April 03	3.93	0.09	0.83	0.10	0.00	0.59	0.01	0.26	0.02
May 03	15.24	0.13	0.57	0.12	0.00	1.95	0.02	0.43	0.01

d^{13}C ratio

	Mean				STDV				
time	Site 1: sediment-free ice	Site 1: water	Site 2: Sediment-laden ice	Site 2: water	Site 1: sediment-free ice	Site 1: water	Site 2: Sediment-laden ice	Site 2: water	Beaufort Sea water
April 02	-20.4	-25.9	-21.5	-24.5	0.20	3.79	0.11	0.15	0.15
Feb 03	-24.9	-23.8	-25.5	-24.9	1.64	0.27	0.44	0.27	0.27
April 03	-23.8	-26.6	-25.8	-28.3	0.95	0.65	0.19	1.73	1.73
May 03	-15.5	-24.3	-24.2	-22.5	0.76	2.72	0.15	1.15	1.15

Table 7:   Vertical temperature gradient at site 1 and 2 in 2003.

		Site 1				Site 2	
Depth (cm)	Febr	Apr	May	Depth (cm)	Feb	Apr	May
air	-29.7	-14.6	1.5	air	-25.4	-14.3	0.8
snow surface	-27.8		0.1	snow surface	-24.2	-13.1	-0.1
snow bottom	-25.4		-0.2	snow bottom	-20.9	-14.6	-0.4
5	-25	-13	-0.8	5	-16.8	-12.4	-0.2
15	-24.5	-11.6	-1.6	15	-14.8	-12.6	-1
25	-20.7	-11	-1.7	25	-12.4	-12.1	-1.4
35	-17.1	-9.8	-1.6	35	-10.5	-11.4	-1.8
45	-14.7	-8.9	-1.5	45	-9.1	-10.3	-1.8
55	-13.5	-7.9	-1.5	55	-6.7	-10.3	-1.8
65	-11.3	-7.4	-1.9	65	-4.6	-9.4	-2
75	-9.5	-6.2	-1.5	75	-3.4	-8.6	-2
85	-8.4	-5.2	-1.4	85		-7.6	-2
95	-6.1	-4.5	-1.3	95		-7.2	-2
110	-5.7	-3.8	-1.1	110		-7.1	-1.8
115	-4.5	-2.8	-0.8	115		-5.3	-1.7
125			-0.8	125		-5.2	-1.8
135			-1.3	135		-4.9	-1.6
				145		-3.6	-1.5
				155		-2.7	-1.5
				165		-1.86	-1.4
				172			-1.4

Data Appendix II

Digital images for the FlowCam Analysis

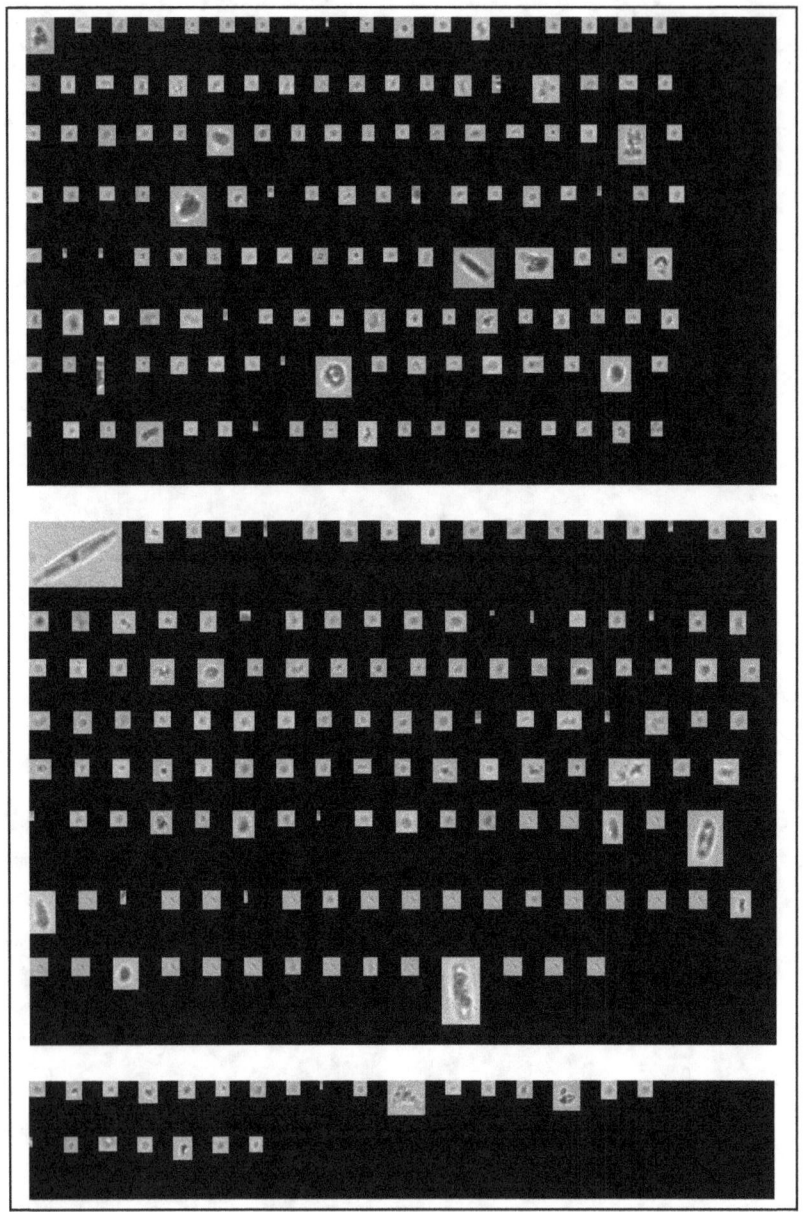

Site 1: February 2003, Sea ice 2

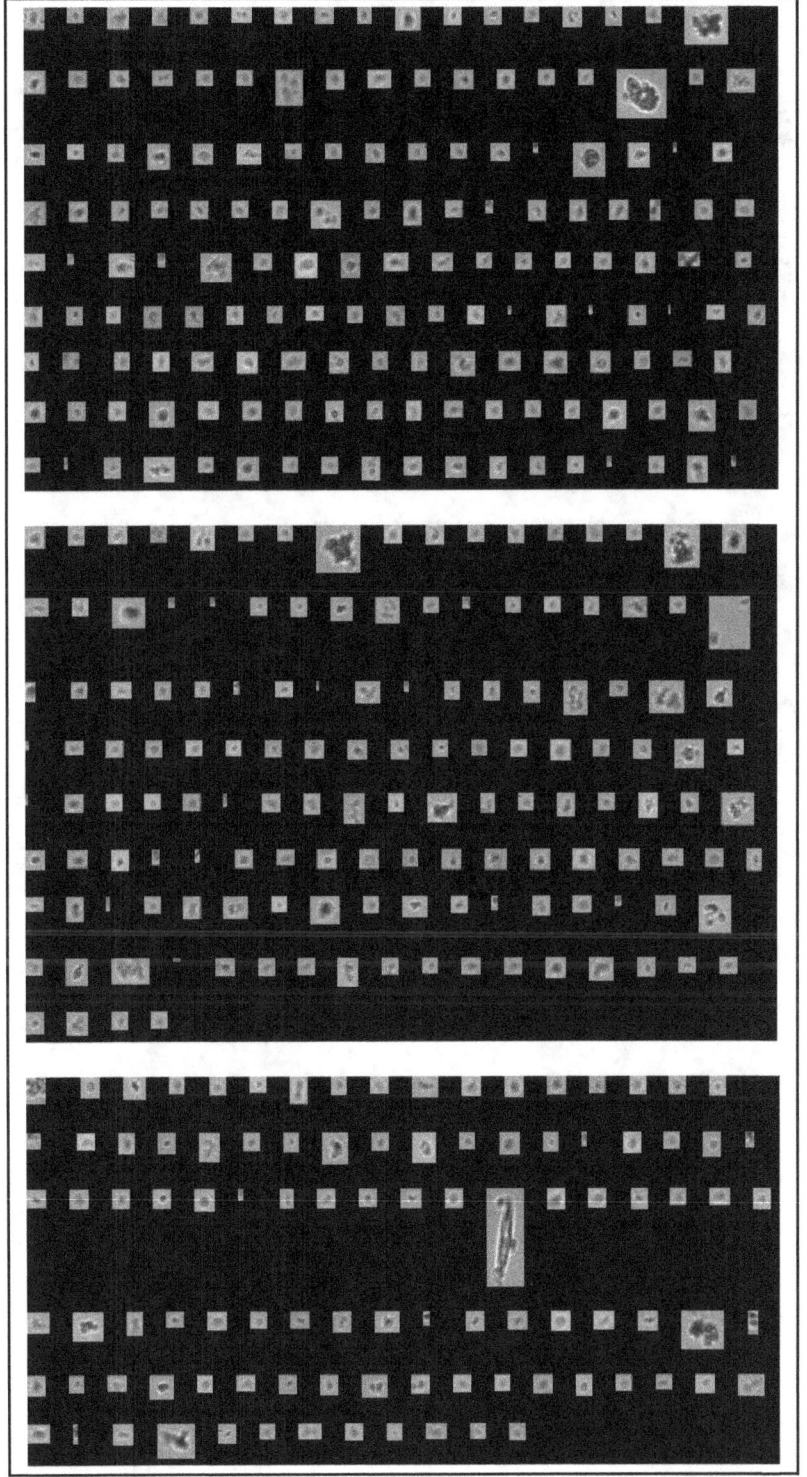

Site 1: February 2003, Sea ice 3

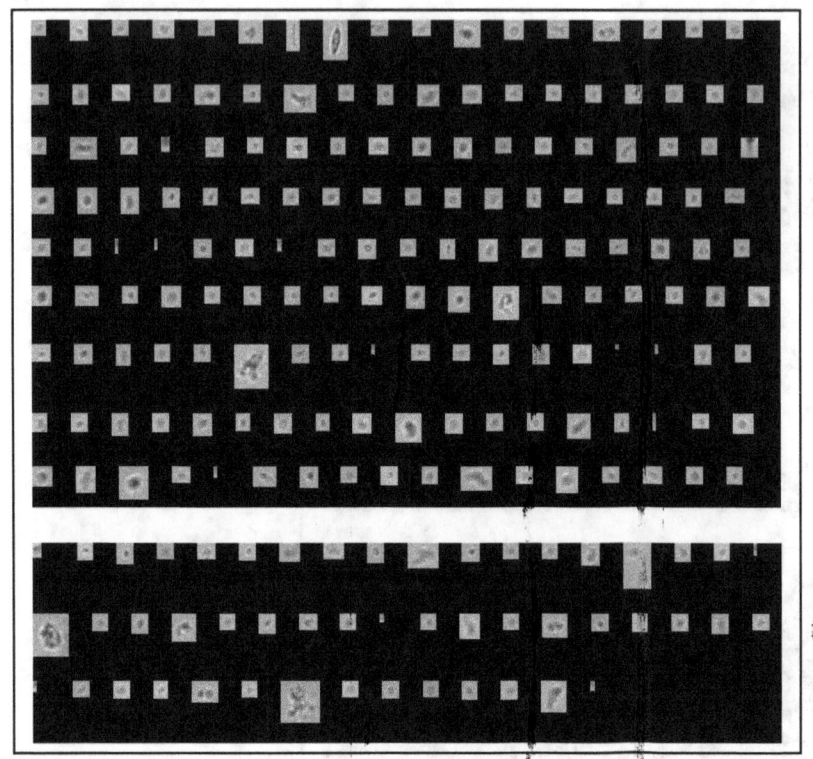

Site 1: February 2003, Sea ice, 4

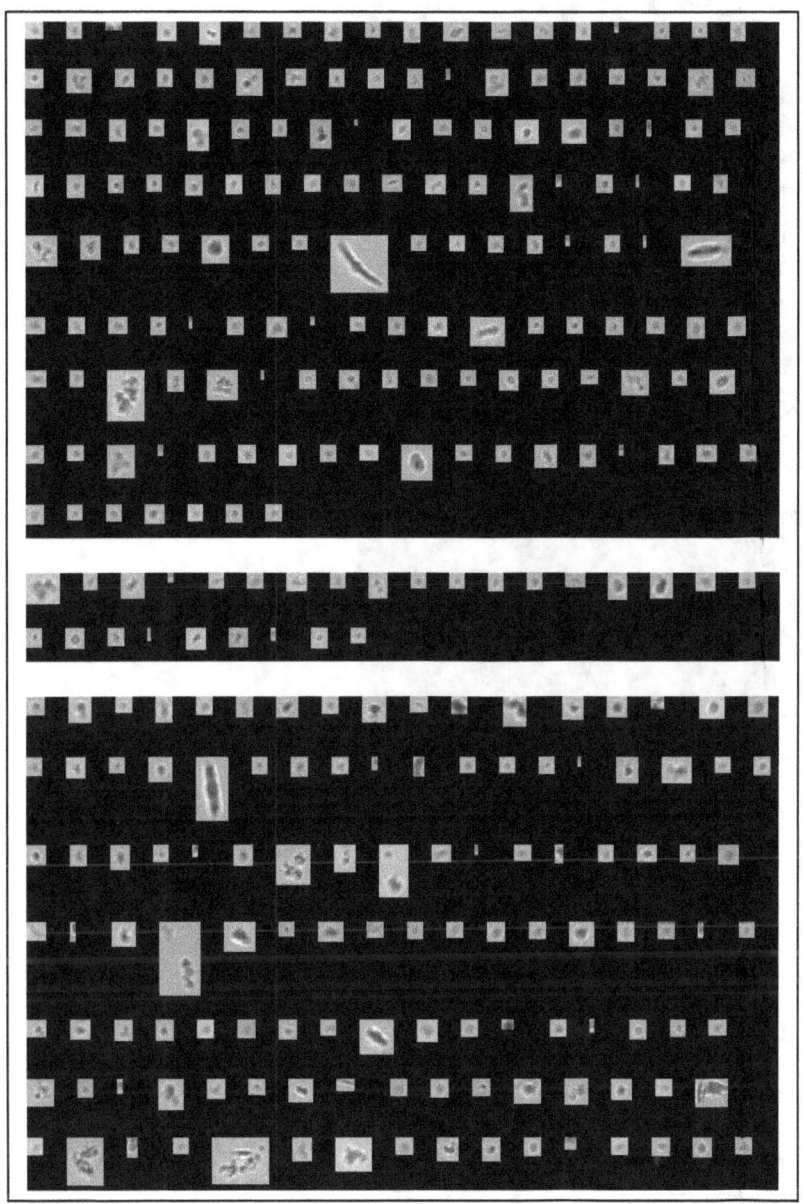

Site 1: February 2003, Water 1

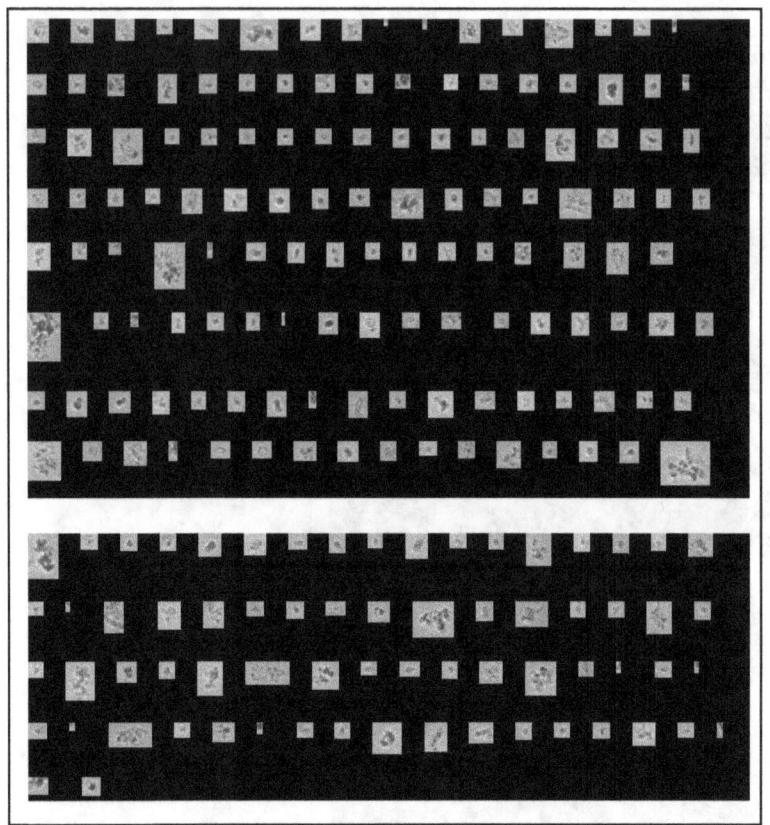

Site 1: February 2003 Water 2

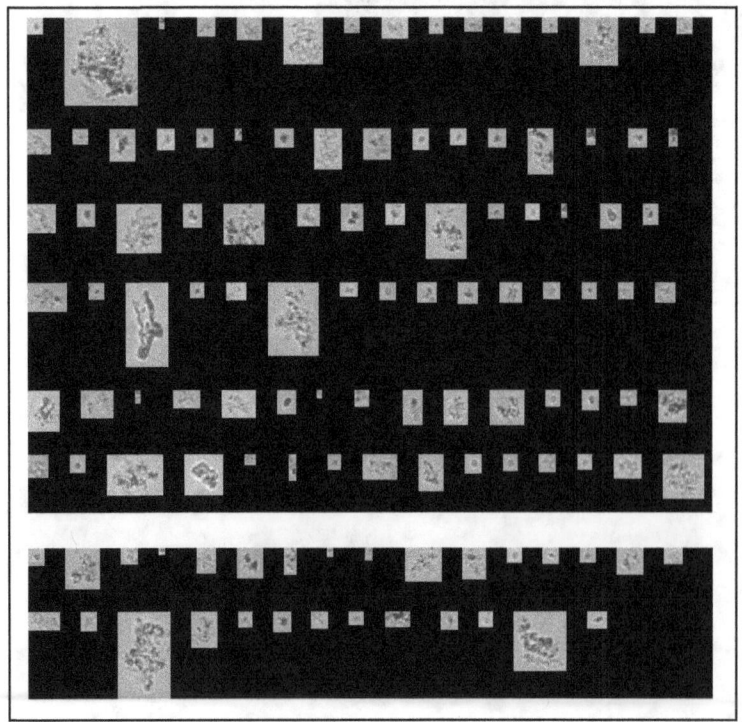

Site 1: February 2003 Water 3

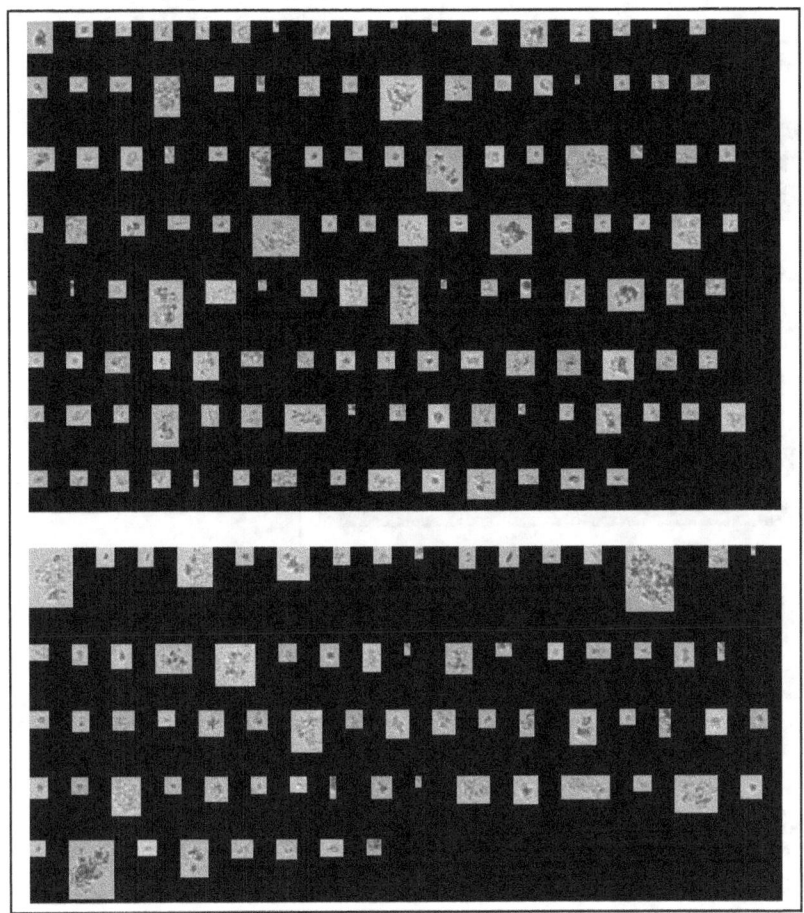

Site 1: February 2003, Water 4

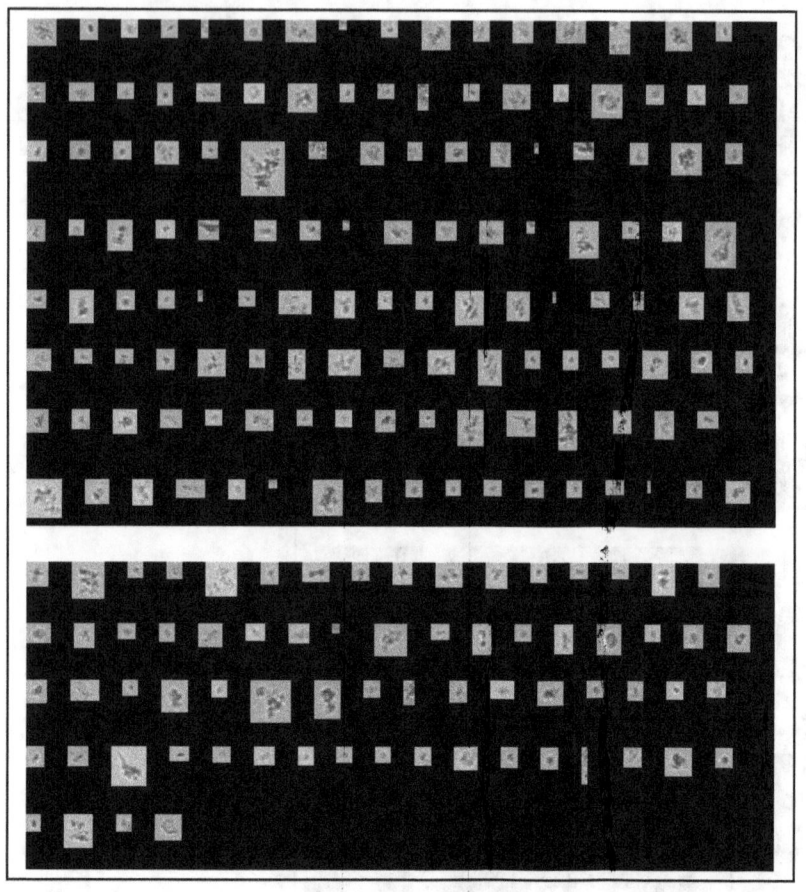

Site 1: May 2003, Sea ice 1

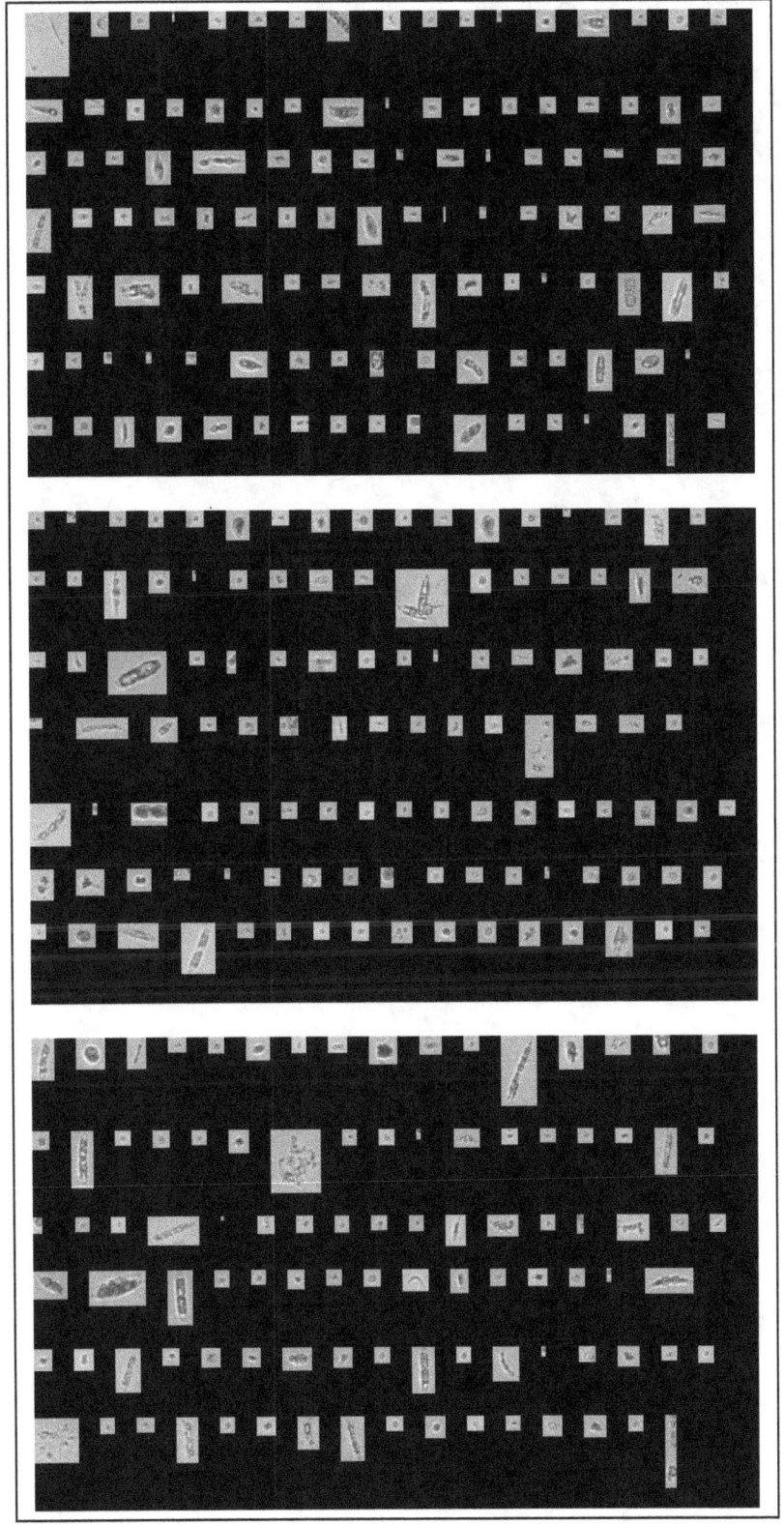

Site 1: May 2003, Sea ice 1 contin.

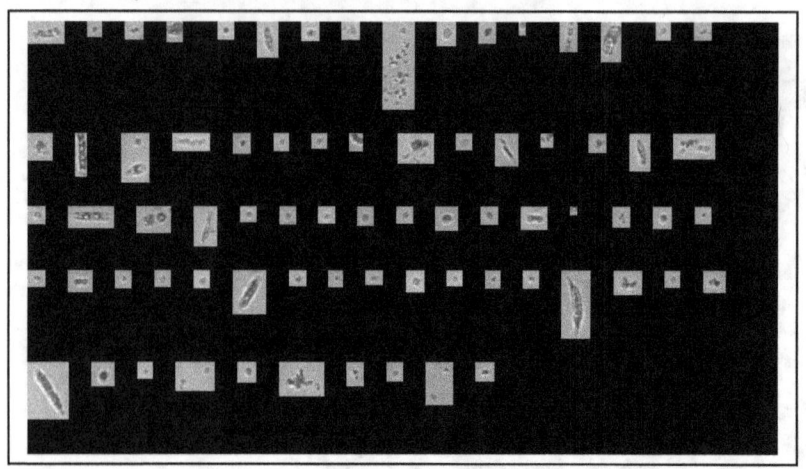

Site 1: May 2003, Sea ice 2

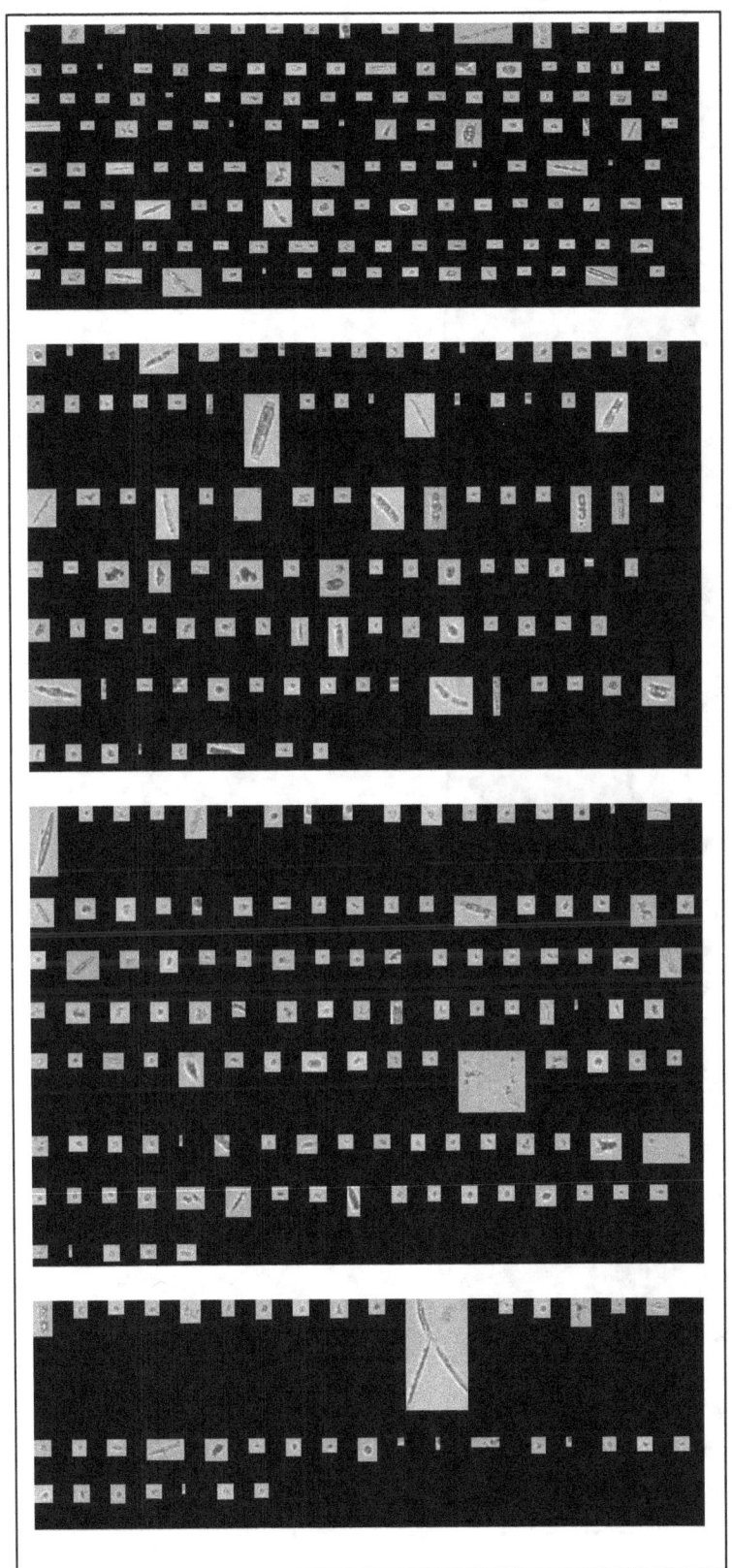

Site 1: May 2003, Sea ice 3

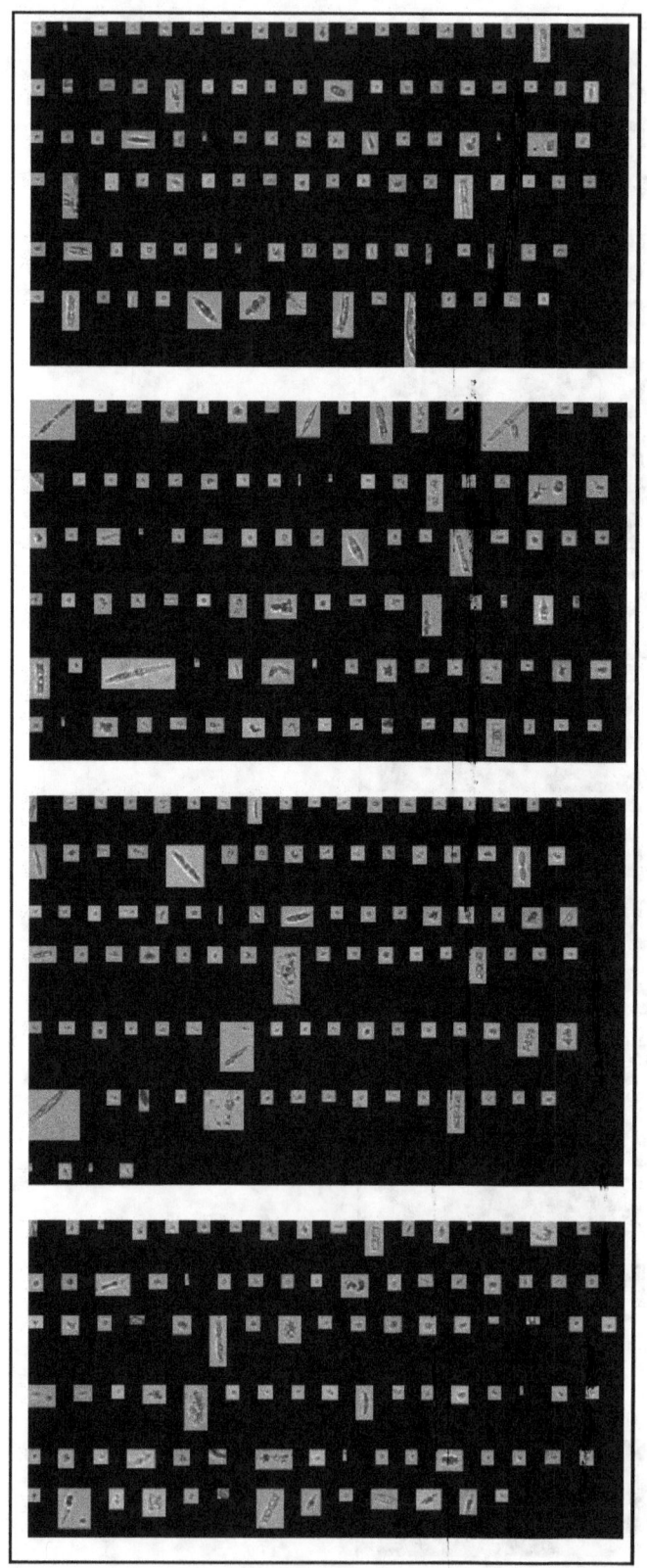

Site 1: May 2003, Water 1

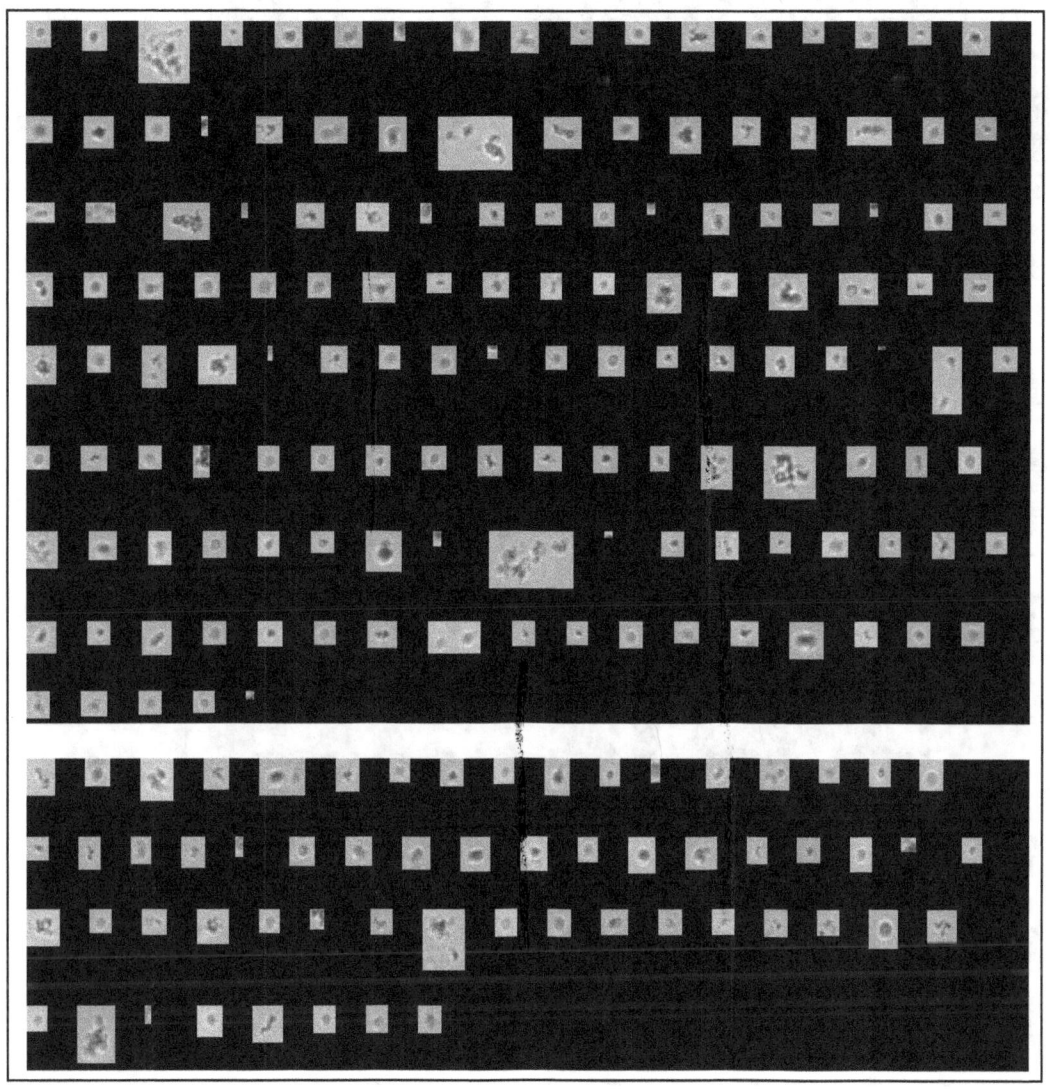

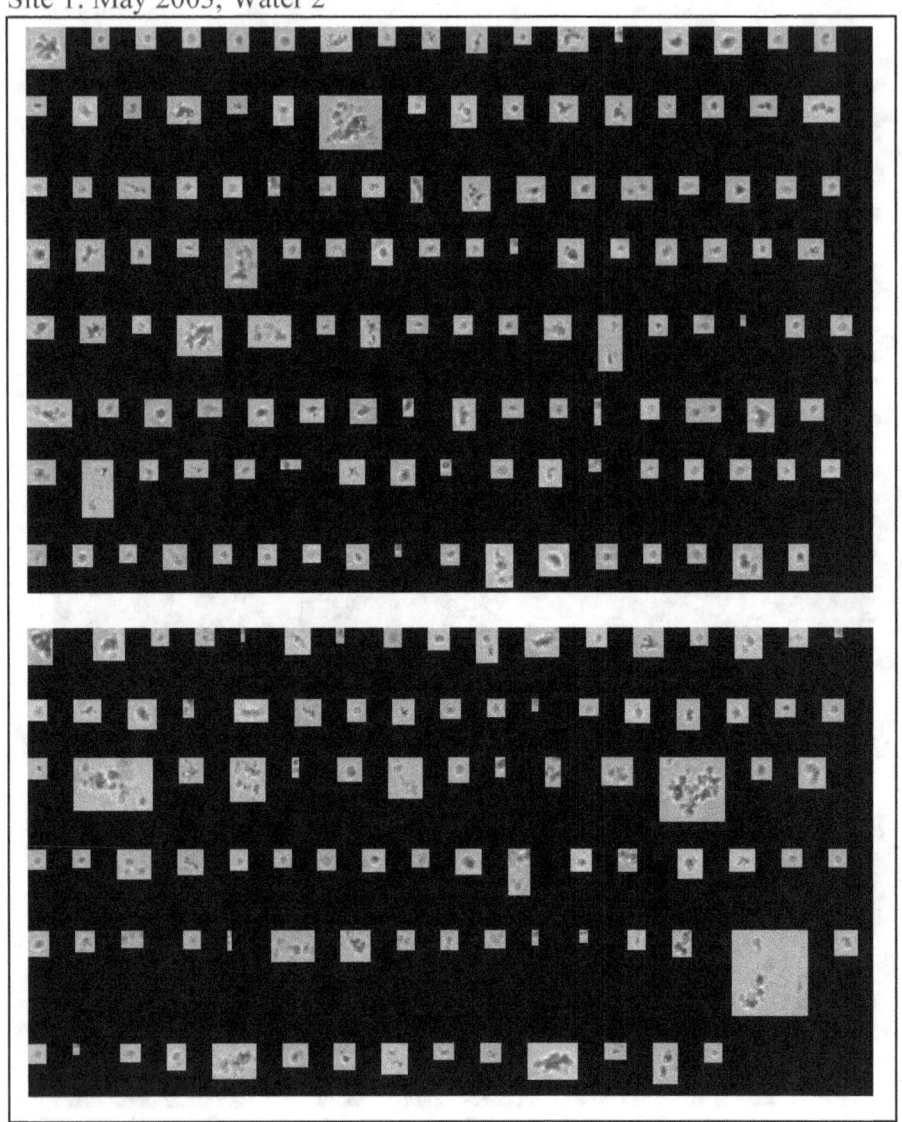

Site 1: May 2003, Water 3

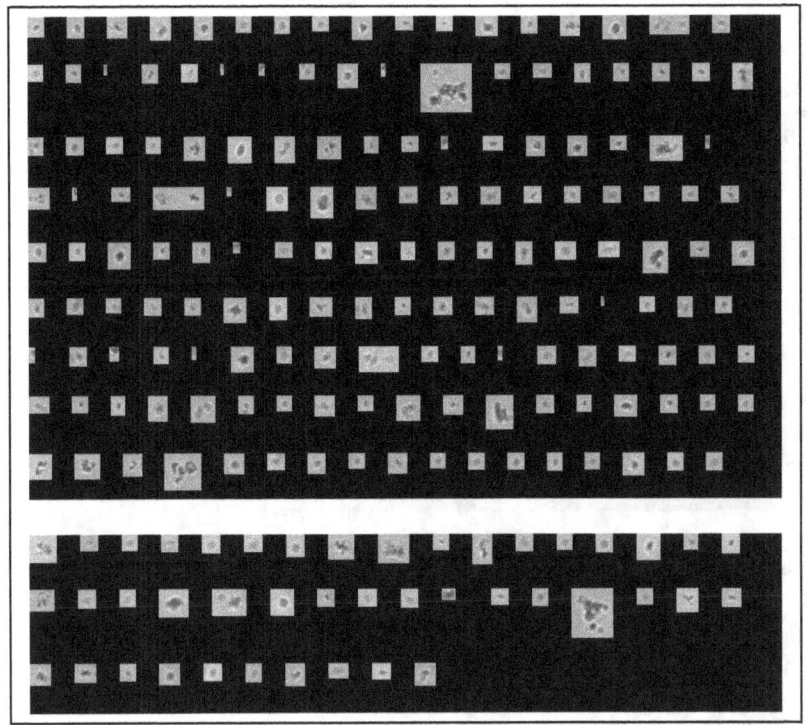

Site 1: May 2003, Water 4

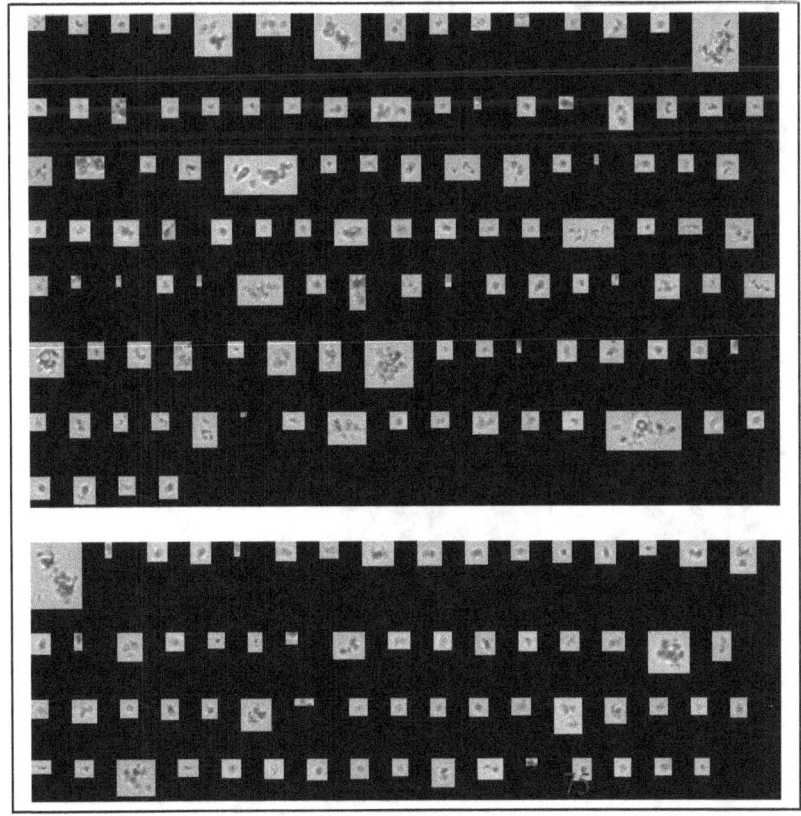

Site 2: February 2003, Sea ice 1

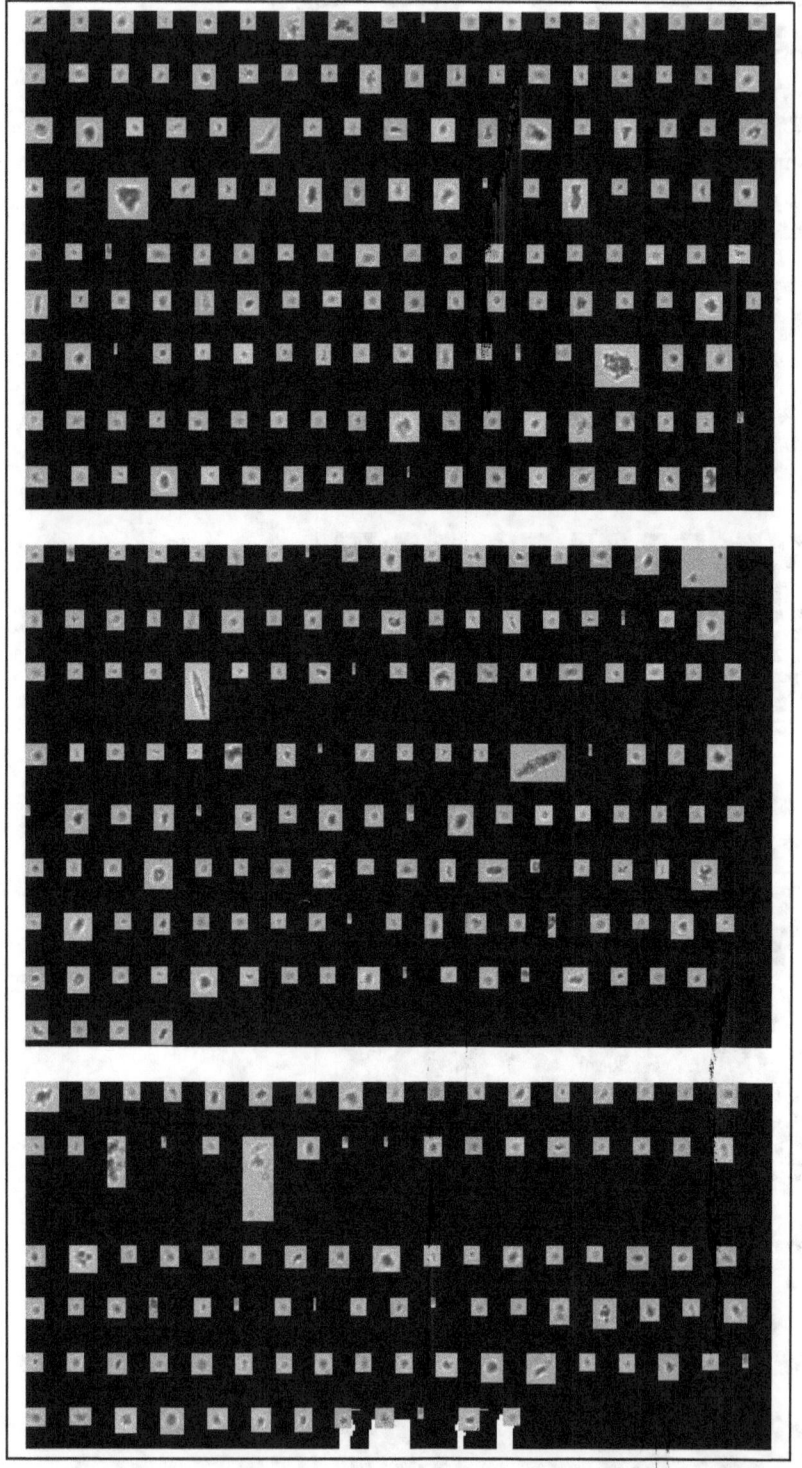

Site 2: February 2003, Sea ice 2

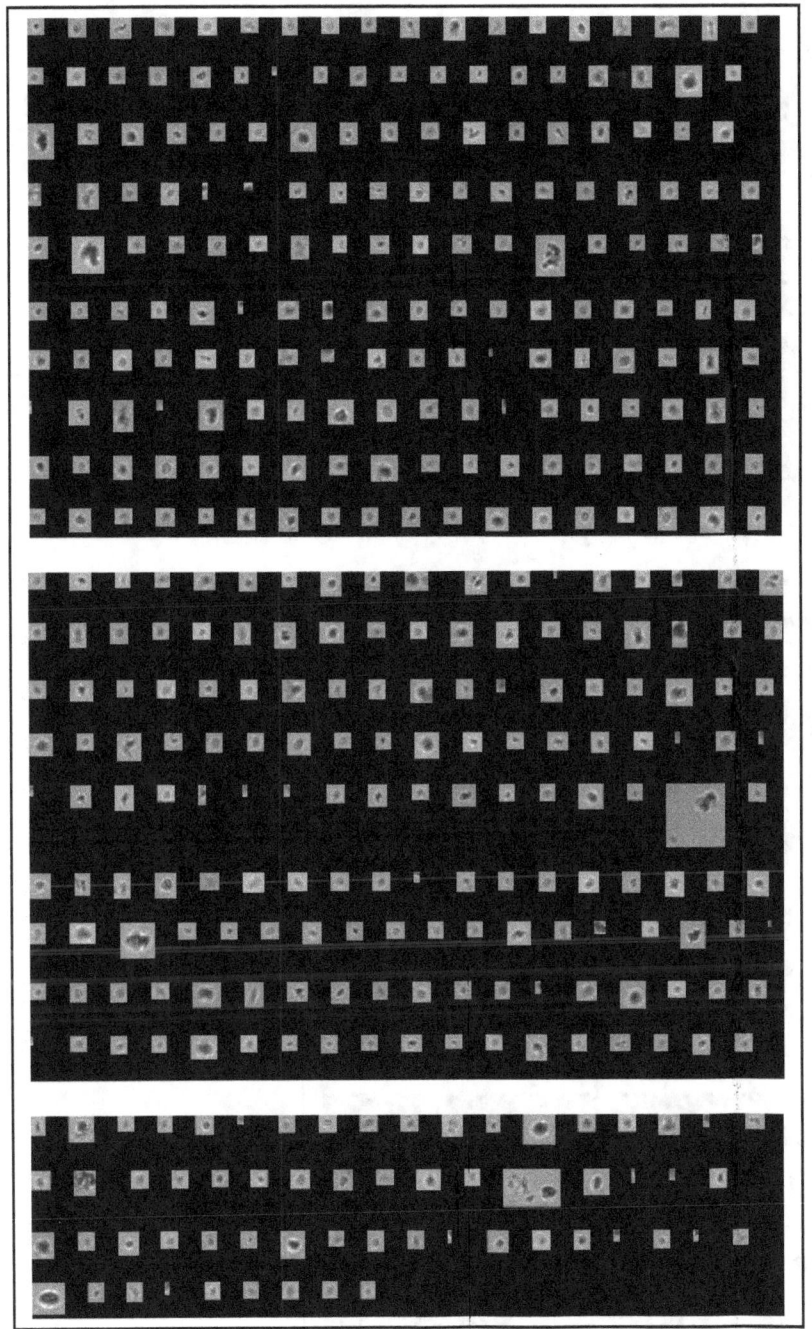

Site 2: February 2003, Sea ice 3

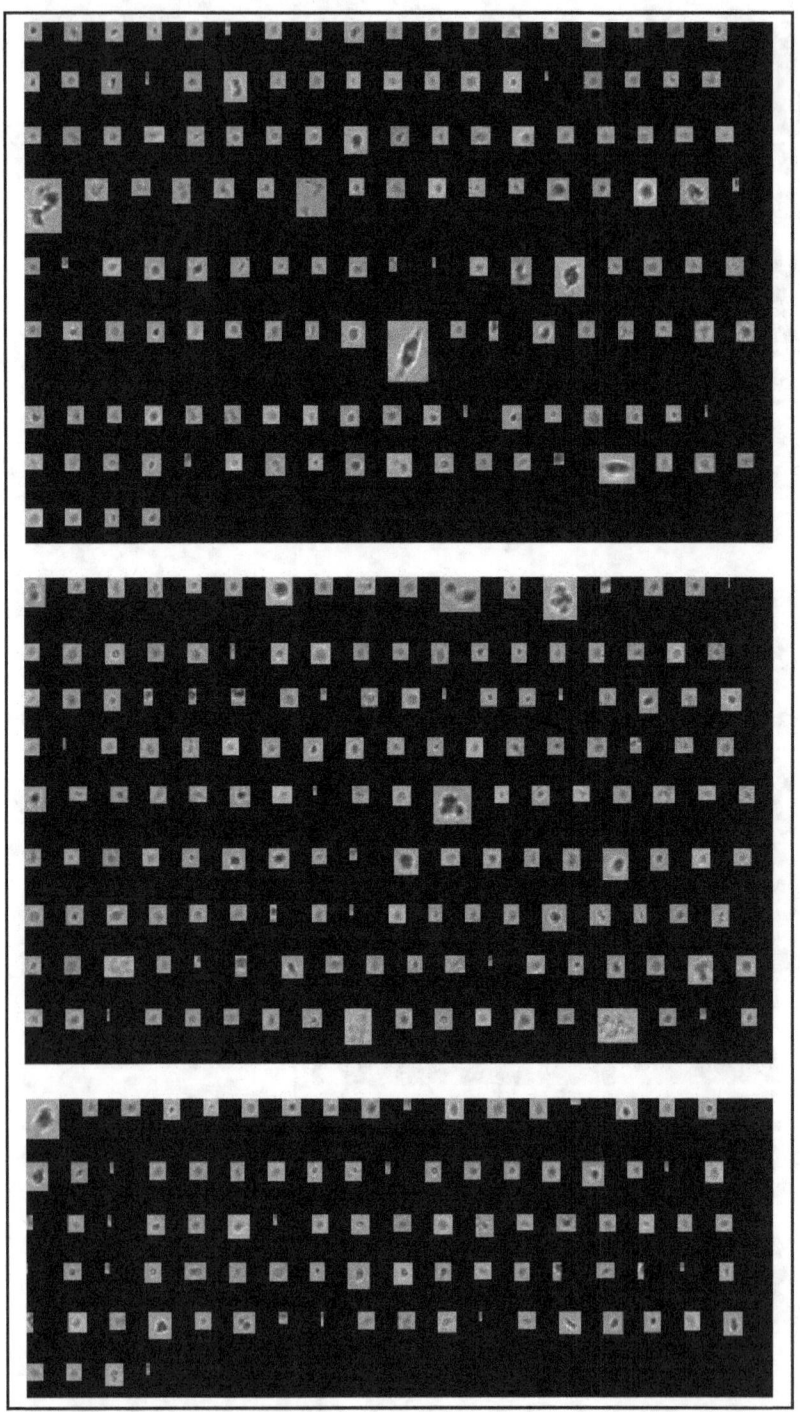

Site 2: February 2003, Sea ice 4

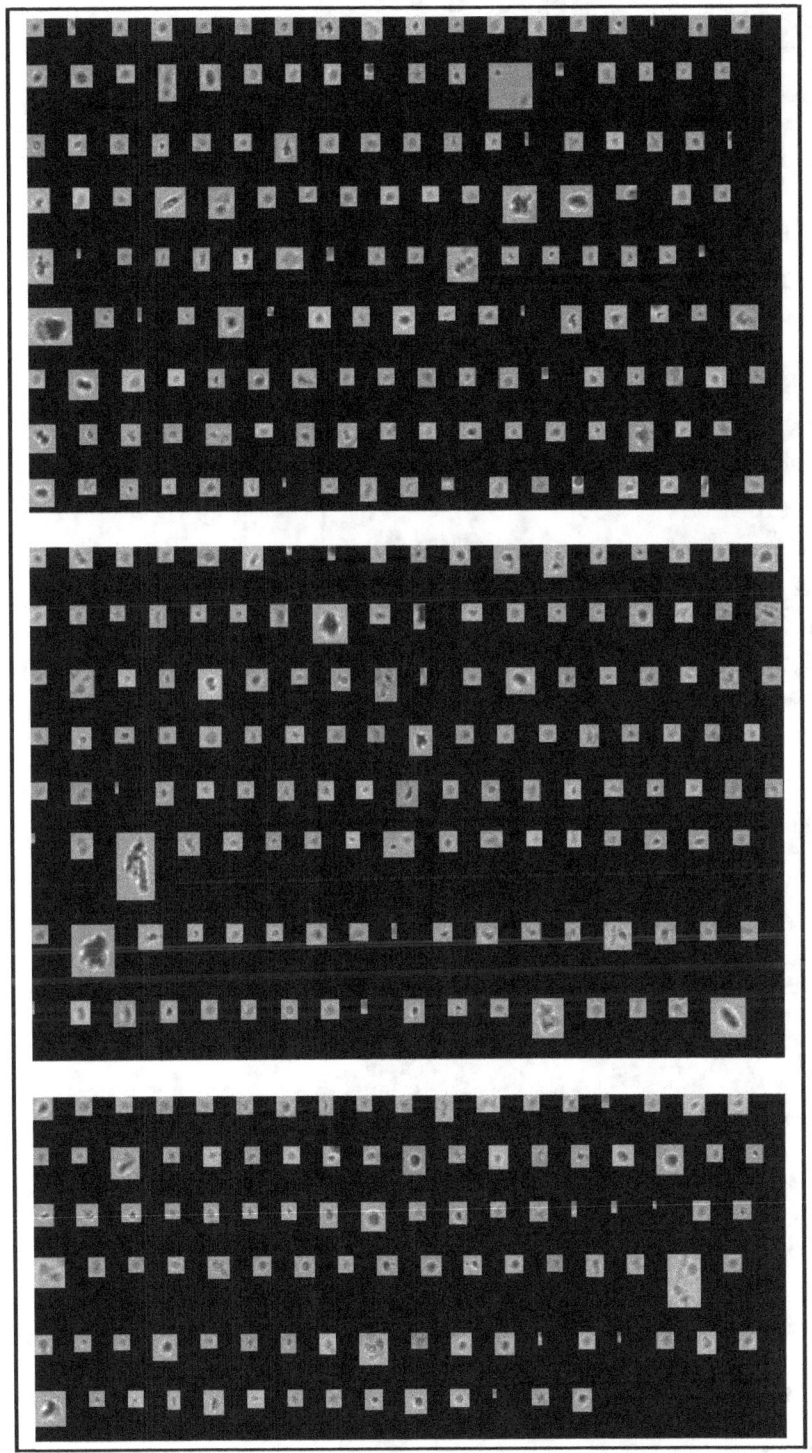

Site 2: February 2003, Water 1

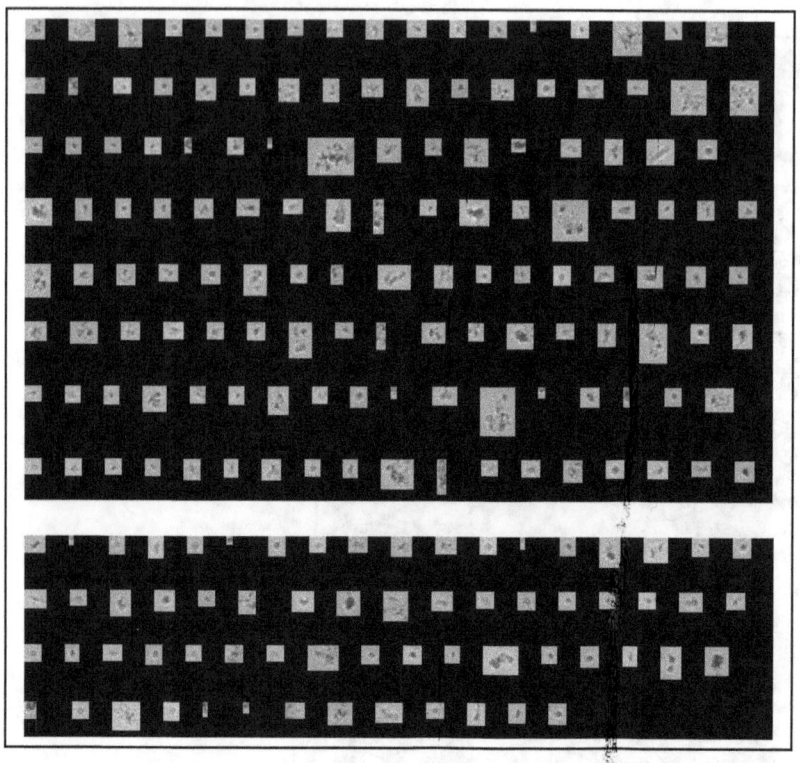

Site 2: February 2003, Water 2

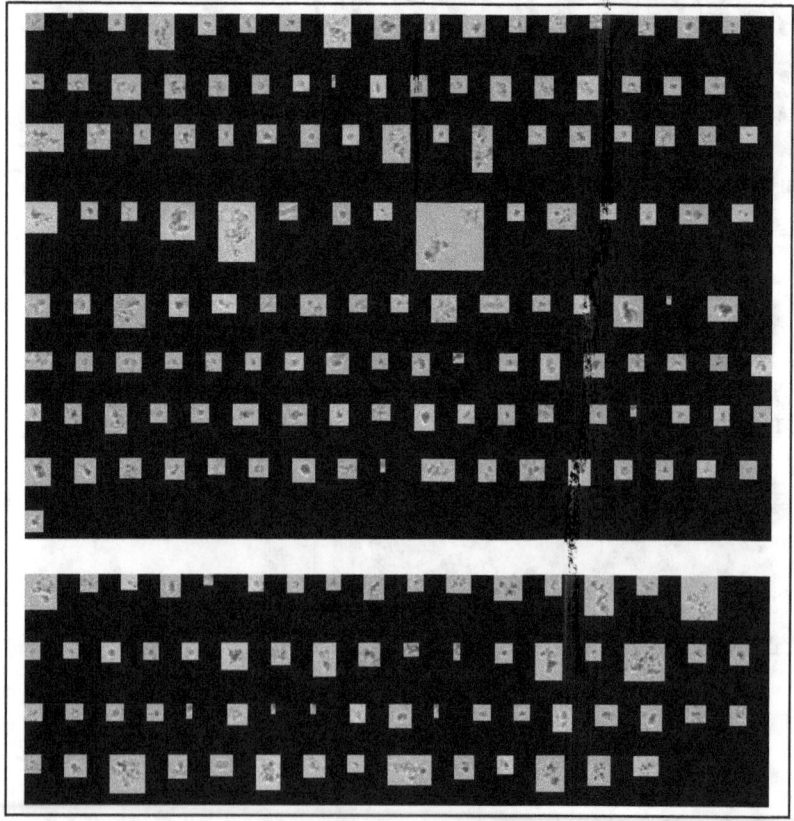

Site 2: February 2003, Water 3

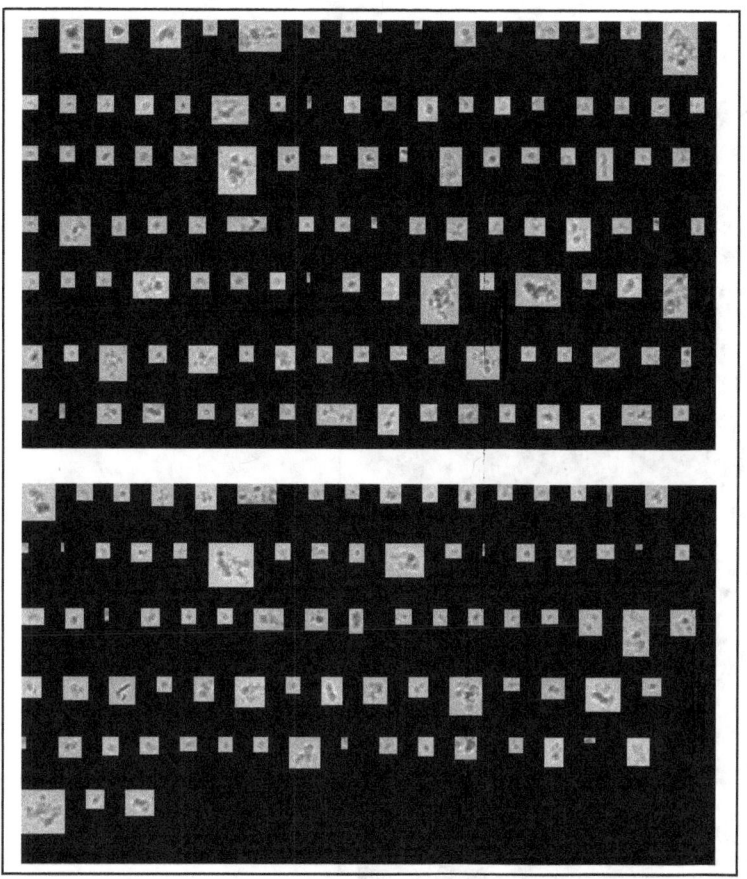

Site 2: February 2003, Water 4

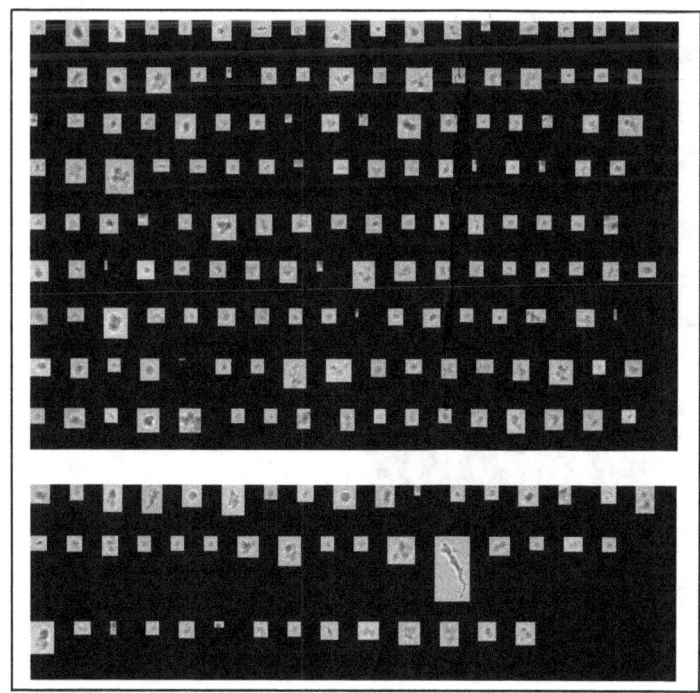

Site 2: May 2003, Sea ice 1

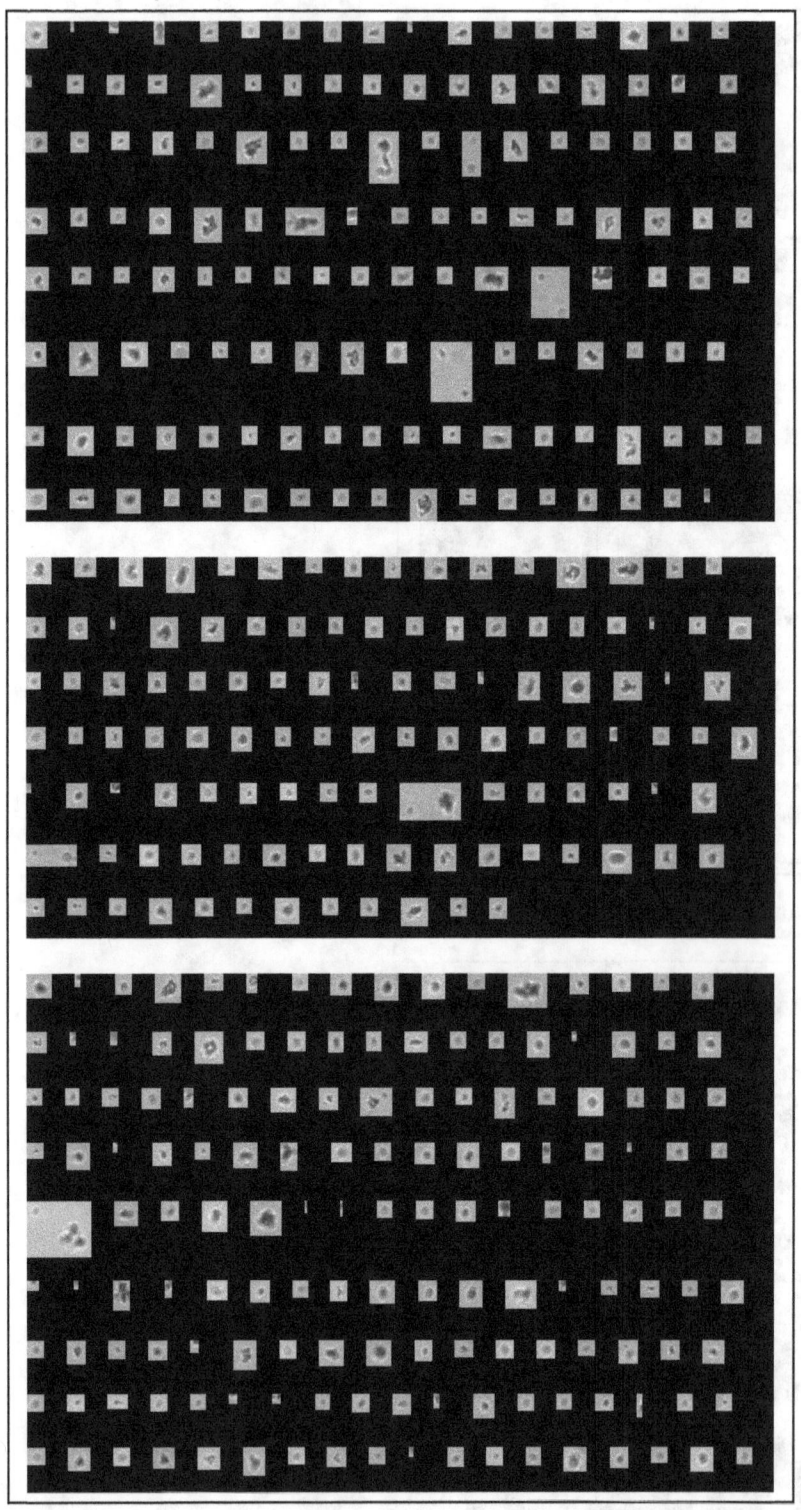

Site 2: May 2003, Sea ice 2

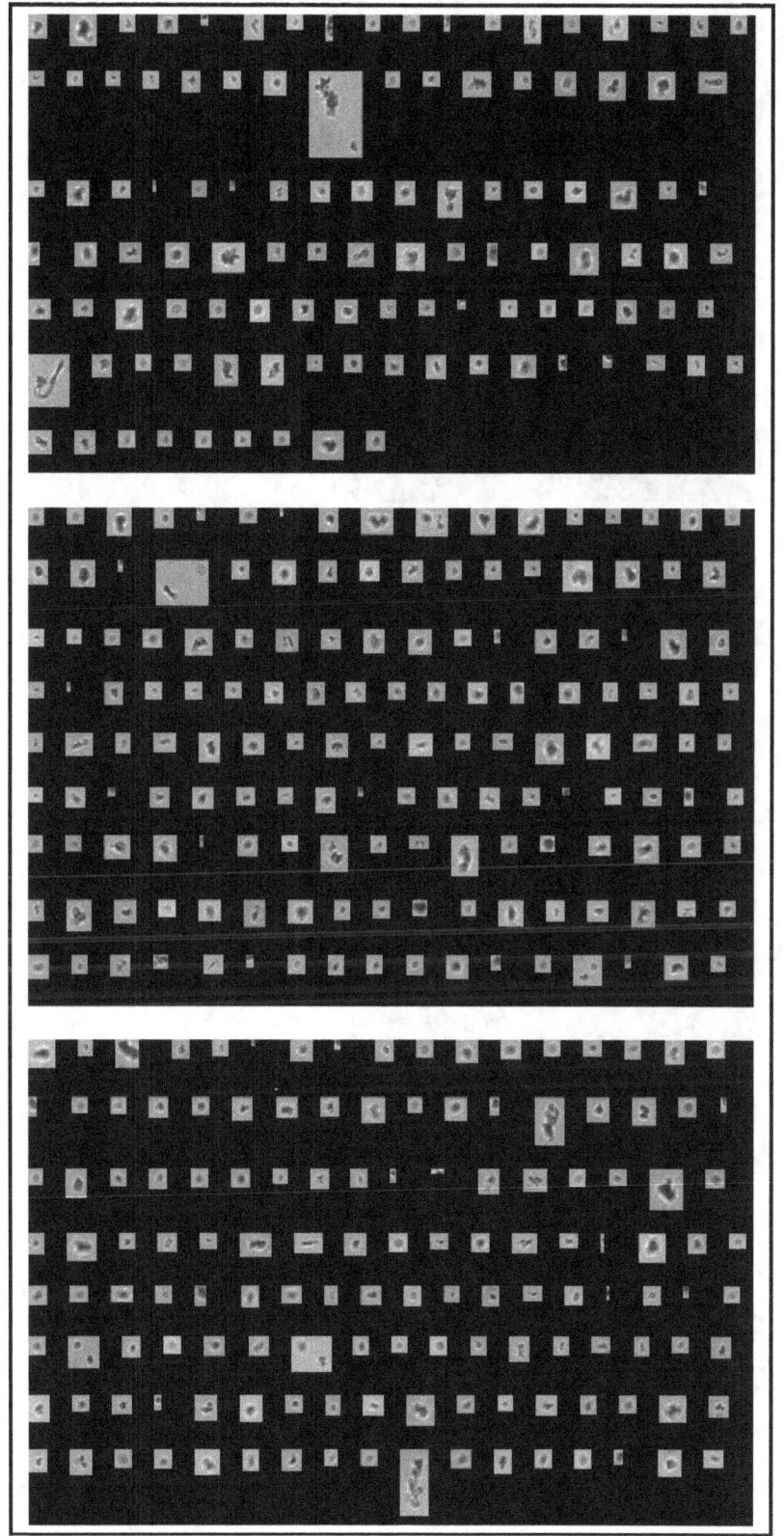

Site 2: May 2003, Sea ice 3

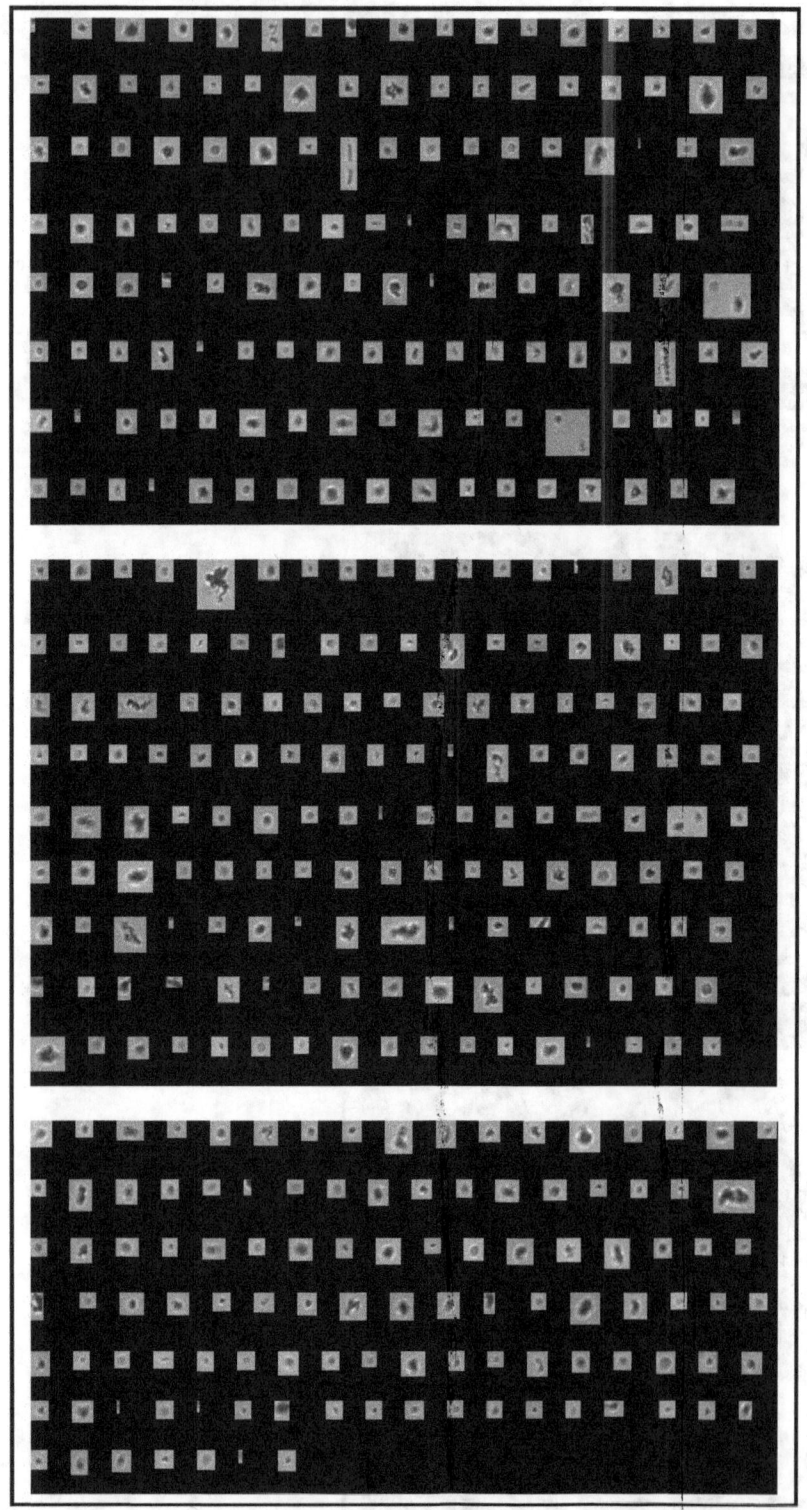

Site 2: May 2003, Sea ice 4

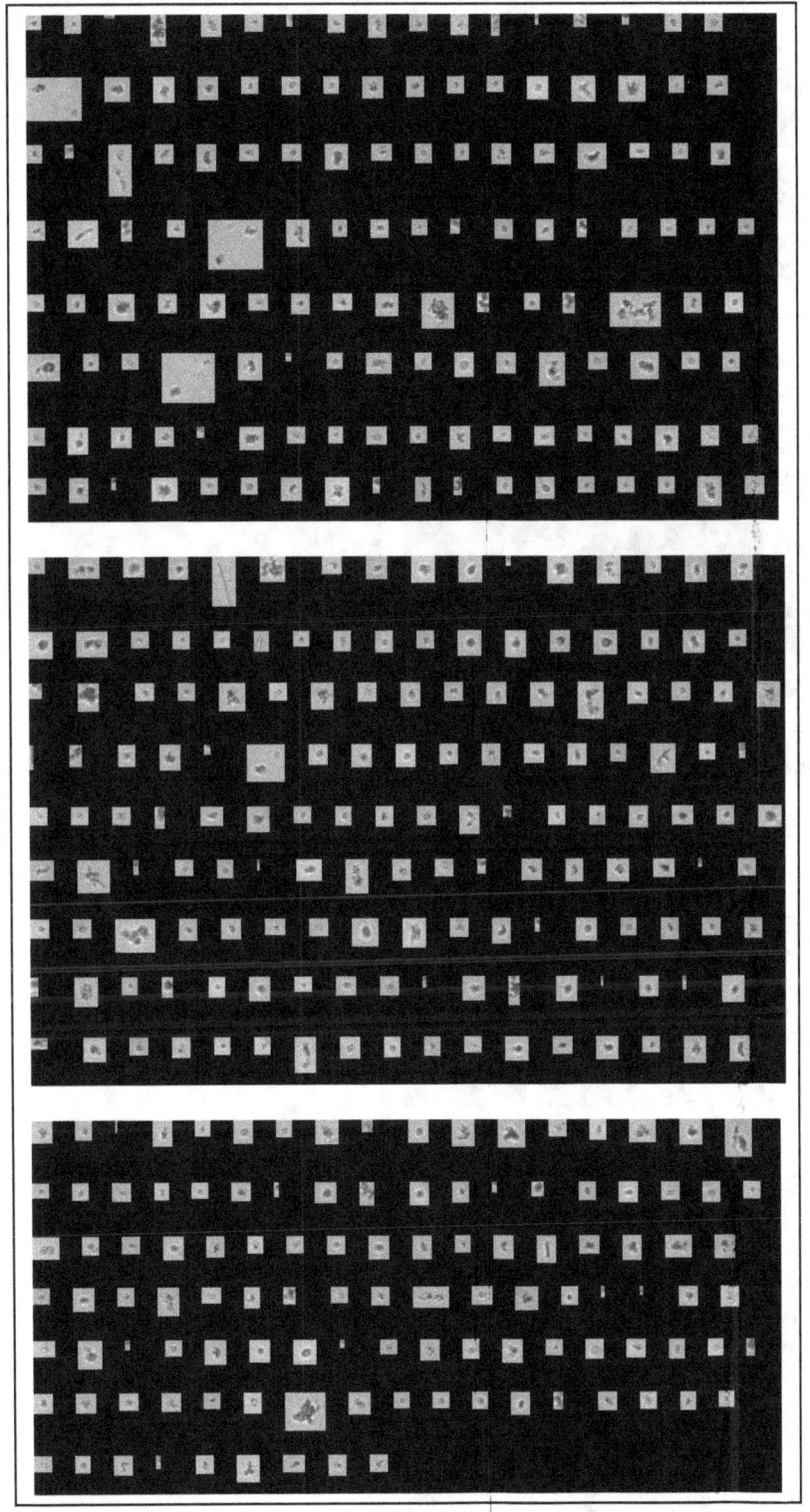

Site 2: Mary 2003, Water 1

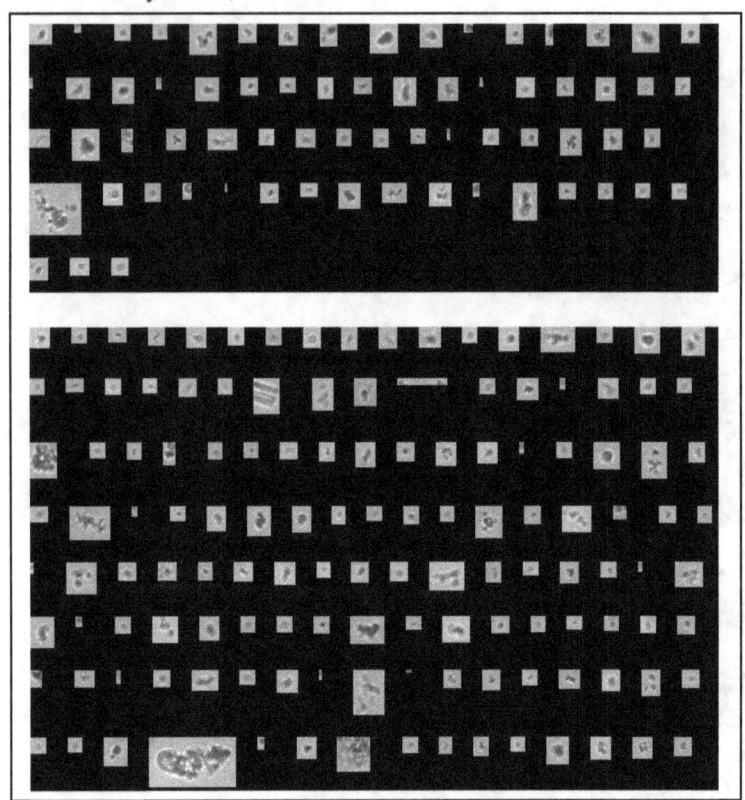

Site 2: Mary 2003, Water 2

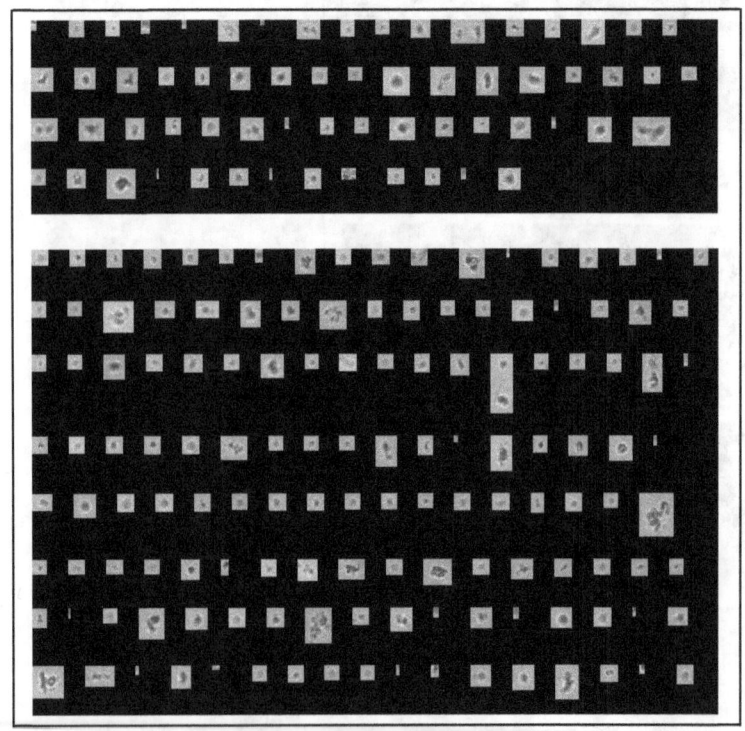

Site 2: May 2003, Water 3

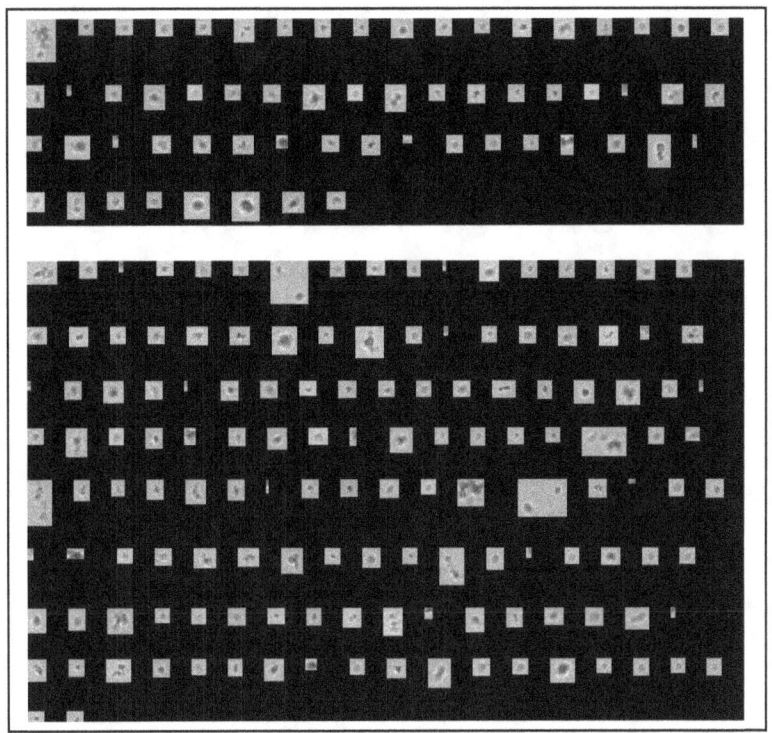

Site 2: May 2003, Water 4

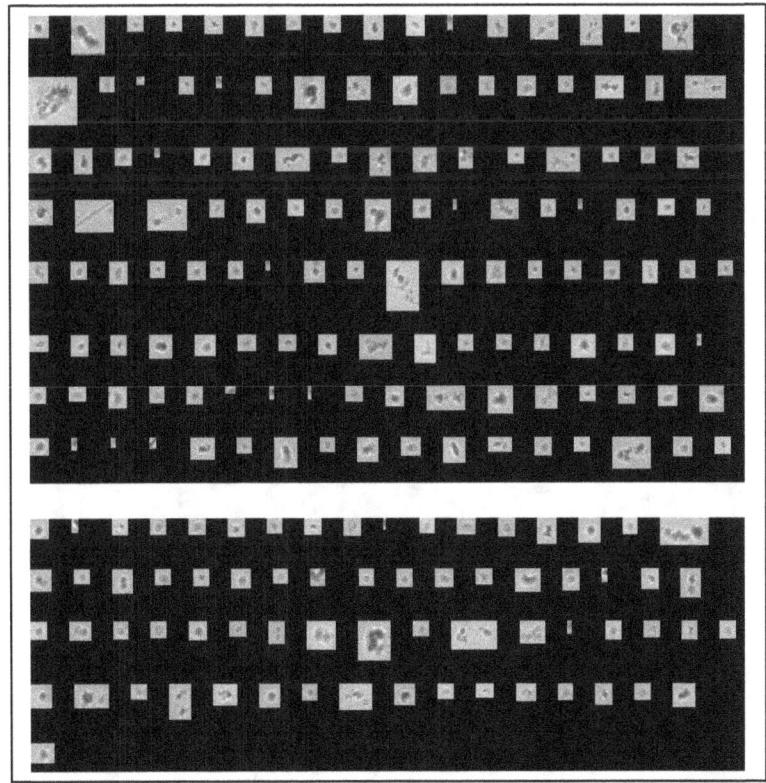